THE LEADERSHIP LIBRARY
V O L U M E   1 1
MAKING THE MOST OF MISTAKES

THE LEADERSHIP LIBRARY

Volume

11

Making the Most of Mistakes

James D. Berkley

Carol Stream, Illinois

WORD BOOKS
PUBLISHER
WACO, TEXAS

A DIVISION OF
WORD, INCORPORATED

Library of Congress Cataloging in Publication Data

Berkley, James D., 1950-
Making the Most of Mistakes

(The Leadership Library; v. 11)
1. Pastoral theology.   I. Title.   II. Series.
BV4011.B49   1987   253   86-33417
ISBN 0-917463-15-3

Printed in the United States of America

To my mother,
Erma Van Meter Berkley,
from whom I first learned
Grace: "It's okay to make a mistake"
and
Law: "But don't let it happen again!"
I'm working on it.

C O N T E N T S

INTRODUCTION

The man who makes no mistakes does not usually make anything.

BISHOP W. C. MAGEE

"Don't just stand there — *do* something!" In most instances, that isn't bad advice. Doing something — anything — often beats doing nothing. But it also leads to mistakes.

Pastors and church leaders are rarely do-nothing people. We busy ourselves with projects and events, programs and visions. We don't want to let grass grow under our feet; there's too much to be done to move the church forward, to help people, to care for needs, and to fulfill pastoral dreams. So we hustle around doing things — and inevitably end up making mistakes.

By *mistakes* I mean everything from little goofs like forgetting a name to major disasters like splitting a church over an unnecessary dispute. Although honest accidents differ greatly from calculated sin, for the sake of simplicity, I'll use the single word *mistake* to refer to all failures of varying proportion and culpability. Had we the wisdom and will and wits, none of us would suffer any of these mistakes. But we don't, so we do.

I'll never forget the wedding I nearly destroyed. As a young pastor, I had just completed a week-long bicycle trip, pushing my way down the California coast with our high school group. My mind had been on devotionals and bent spokes and headwinds — not on my calendar. We logged our final twenty miles before church on Sunday, riding into the church parking lot ten minutes before the service. Following the service I tumbled into bed, exhausted.

Just as I dissolved into sleep, the phone rang: "Uh, are you Reverend Berkley?"

"Yes, I am."

"Aren't you supposed to be doing a wedding?"

Suddenly every bad dream I'd had of leaving a couple stewing at the altar played in my imagination. It's a sick feeling. "I'll be there in fifteen minutes."

Actually it took me closer to twenty minutes to throw on some clothes, race to the church for my robe, and gun my car to the summit of the park overlooking Ventura. But I was lucky. I arrived to find a happy knot of people enjoying the balmy summer day and apparently unconcerned with my inexcusable tardiness. With my face several shades redder than normal, I launched into the service.

Driving home after refusing the honorarium, I counted my blessings. *What if it had been a large, formal wedding party waiting impatiently in a hot sanctuary, and they couldn't reach me?* I shudder yet at the thought.

Some mistakes have greater consequences than others. The bride could have been the daughter of an influential board member who didn't like me anyway. Or the senior pastor could have been searching for the conclusive reason to ask for my resignation. Or the best man could have punched me in the nose. I was fortunate. I can only hope the consequences of all my mistakes turn out as benign. But they probably won't.

Mistakes cause consequences. Pastors have found their belongings stacked on the parsonage porch for lesser crimes against the church. One pastor was fired on the spot for "being too involved in the church." His fatal "mistake"? Adjusting the thermostat!

Many a church leader has spent agonizing months trying to "what-if" a ministry miscue: *What if I had held my temper? What if I had remembered to consult Dorothy?* Ministry mistakes can become serious in short order. Most are no laughing matter.

I have kicked myself over the snap color choice that gave our church in Dixon a two-tone roof — that leaked to boot! Upon word of her death, I have sorrowed over my failure to visit a hospitalized parishioner. I have totally flopped in a counseling situation with a rebellious teenager. I have contributed to the "short-gevity" of part-time staff members by deficient supervision. Certainly I've made my share of mistakes as a pastor.

And so have we all. Perhaps you've lost your effectiveness and been asked to resign. Maybe you conceded a theological battle you should have won. Likely there are episodes you would just as soon forget. Whether humorous faux pas or drastic errors, your mistakes follow you throughout ministry and color your personality and potential.

So what can we do about mistakes? We can't avoid them. We can't even sidestep all the consequences. But we can take an honest look at these occurrences and see how we can make the best of less-than-perfect circumstances.

Once made, mistakes do suggest better or worse resolution. With few truly unique mistakes and with pastors adding to the pool of experience daily, surely there is something to be learned about mistakes — something that can help all of us trip less often and avoid a drastic fall when we do. Perhaps we can even *benefit* from the mistakes we do make.

That is the purpose of this book. I haven't made all the mistakes yet, although I'm working on it. I'm writing more as a scribe relating what others have dictated than as a scholar sharing some vast knowledge of "flubology." Wise and resourceful pastors have erred in the practice of ministry. They've goofed; they've tripped hard in some cases. But they've survived. They've even grown from the experience. This book will attempt to bring their experience and insight to the fore.

Since we will invariably make mistakes, we might as well have the resources to do it with as much grace as possible.

Mistakes — even failure — need not be the end, but rather the beginning. If experience is a schoolmaster, mistakes can be our professors. We can be the better for them.

Woody Allen says, "If you're not failing now and again, it's a sign you're playing it safe." Perhaps we can take that one step further: If you're not learning from your mistakes, it's a sign you're due for more than your share of them as you take the inevitable risks of ministry.

THE PRINCE TURNED PAUPER

There is no fiercer hell than the failure in a great object.

JOHN KEATS

Not one of the scores of young couples I have counseled prior to their wedding expected *their* marriage to fail. Others' maybe, but not theirs. After all, they loved each other. They, of all couples, would stay together.

Yet, some have divorced.

In the same way, no pastor kneels at ordination — those many hands conferring God's strength — expecting to fail in ministry, or even to stumble. Certainly mistakes are possible. Yes, other pastors have taken a tumble. But not *this* pastor! No, this one loves the Lord. He is called into ministry. She is gifted by the Spirit. Everything appears promising.

Yet just such pastors — devout, earnest, gifted, prayerful — wind up removing their certificate of ordination from the wall and scanning the help-wanted ads in the Sunday paper. They have committed seemingly fatal errors, and their ministry died aborning. Left with a heavy bookshelf and a heavier heart, they wonder, *What did I do wrong?*

Although not all mistakes prove fatal to ministry, every one carries a price tag. Blunders severely limit one's effectiveness. They cause painful setbacks requiring years to remedy. They close doors and dash dreams. They may even dishonor God.

No one *wants* to make mistakes. Yet no one is immune.

Pastors and church leaders venture out, and some of them fall hard — some you would least expect.

Gordon Weekley was one such pastor. From all indications, Gordon appeared destined to preside as a prince of the church. He was born into a godly home in Atlanta, the heart of the Bible Belt. His home church, First Baptist, was pastored by a statesman of the denomination who later became Gordon's seminary president, "and he had a great influence on me," Gordon recalls.

Gordon's path to ordination led him to college at Furman University and seminary at Southern Baptist in Louisville. After seminary, Gordon pastored two small churches in North Carolina, and then, in 1955, accepted a call to Charlotte to become the first pastor of the fledgling Providence Baptist Church. As Gordon put it, "They had a dream, eight acres, and that was it." But Gordon went to work with his twenty-six people, determined to build a congregation. In the next thirteen years, 2,200 people joined the church. The prince had a golden touch.

Gordon enjoyed the prosperity of the church. A dedicated worker, he loved forging a new church out of nothing. Immersing himself in a day's work came easily. Maybe too easily. It became nearly a day-and-night obsession.

As the church grew, even with the addition of staff, Gordon kept his frantic pace. "I saw everybody at least once or twice while they were in the hospital. And in the beginning I could, because the congregation was tiny. But I didn't make the transition to a more sensible approach when the church grew to an unwieldy size," Gordon admits.

Yet, even with the killing pace, Gordon loved his ministry. It was all he had ever hoped it would be. His church was growing. Its influence was spreading throughout the Charlotte area. People inside and outside the community were taking notice. Lives were being touched. Obviously, God was blessing the work. Gordon calls those "very happy and exciting years." He was living the pastor's dream.

Gordon enjoyed a warm friendship with a physician in his congregation. Their families were close, too, often piling into a station wagon and heading for the beach together in the summer. One day in 1958, Gordon mentioned to his friend, "Frank, I've got some signs of jitteriness I shouldn't have, and I'm not sleeping well. You know of anything I can do for it?"

Frank thought for a minute and replied, "There's a new drug out, and it's a nonbarbiturate, not habit-forming. I think it might be the very thing for you." He wrote out a prescription.

Gordon tried the new pill that evening and found it did seem to calm him and make him drowsy. But there was an unexpected side effect: a sense of euphoria. Gordon had to admit, he liked it. And the sleep was gratefully received into his fast-paced life.

The next day he awoke more refreshed than he had in weeks. He dove into his work with renewed energy and delight. He didn't have to shut down at supper time; he had the energy to extend his day into the evening. He was pleased to be able to get more done. So pleased, in fact, that he took the pill that next night. It, too, calmed him and produced that euphoric boost. Soon the pill at bedtime became a regular practice.

As the days went by, the evening pill seemed to be doing less and less. The nervousness was surfacing again, and Gordon tossed and turned one night just like before. But not only was the calm passing, that nightly warm sense of joy was diminishing, too. *If one pill makes me feel good, one and a half will make me feel even better,* Gordon thought. So he increased his dosage ever so little, and again basked in that encompassing sense of euphoria. That mistake proved his undoing.

Gordon claims it wasn't the pressure of ministry that caused his problems. He was having such a good time that he wasn't even sure there were pressures. After all, people were coming to know the Lord. Buildings were being built and staff members integrated into the ministry. Gordon rode the Providence Church crest with great satisfaction. He was an accomplished pastor beloved by his growing congregation. Maybe there were pressures, but they were the good kind, the ones resulting from growth and prosperity.

And there were always the pills at the end of the evening to smooth the rough edges and make him feel good. The wonders of medical science!

Frank was a good buddy, and because he was so close to Gordon, he didn't pay that much attention to Gordon's increasing requests for prescription refills. Had Gordon been a stranger, those requests for greater dosages would have sounded an alarm. But Frank trusted Gordon, thinking it only *seemed* a short time ago that he approved the last refill. Gordon learned to play the situation well, and no one knew his problem.

Charlotte is Billy Graham's home town. It was inevitable that the pastor of burgeoning Providence Baptist Church would eventually cross paths with the Graham family. In 1960 Gordon was invited to accompany the Graham team on his African crusade.

Prior to setting out, Gordon went to Frank and said, "I'm going to be over there with all those jungle sounds and all, and you know I'm such a horrible sleeper anyway. Maybe you need to give me a few more of these pills just in case — for this particular trip, anyway. And, uh, we'll be doing a lot of traveling throughout some nights so we can speak during the days."

"Well," Frank replied, "you may need a little something to keep you alert." So unbeknownst to anyone other than his doctor, the promising young pastor observed the African crusade with a pocket full of amphetamines. He found he got a lift from them, too, and he grew to like their mood-changing, mind-altering effect — a lot.

Gordon hadn't sought the euphoria in the first place, nor was it his intent to become hooked on it. His growing dependency on the uppers and downers was the work of what he considered harmless medications. For many months, he couldn't admit that what he was really seeking was the euphoria, or that he was getting hooked on it. Drug addiction and pastoring a successful church just didn't fit together. Princes don't become junkies, do they?

Gordon waltzed this dangerous dance for about six years until Frank's office nurse came to Frank in alarm: "Doctor, don't you think we're authorizing too many of these medications for Reverend Weekley from all these pharmacies?" She produced a record of Gordon's prescriptions from multiple pharmacies.

"*All these pharmacies?*" Frank looked stricken. "Let me see that chart!" He had not been watching Gordon's record. Why should he? If you can't trust your pastor, who can you trust? He'd only wanted to help Gordon, but Gordon, in his continuing need for larger doses, had spread his prescriptions across pharmacies throughout the county.

As soon as Frank examined Gordon's charts, he called him. "Gordon, why didn't you tell me — you're going all over the county to fill those prescriptions! That's how addicts behave. I'm cutting off these prescriptions effective immediately."

"C'mon, Frank," Gordon replied, "you know I need those pills. You prescribed them yourself!" Gordon was wheedling now, but it didn't work. Frank shut the valve, leaving Gordon without the flow of drugs.

So Gordon sought other sources. He was a cagey user. Never did he have to resort to street sales. A distinguished, urbane man, Gordon conned dozens of doctors into writing him a prescription. At one point, Gordon had a string of physicians and pharmacies running from Charlotte to Richmond. Town by town by town, he'd make a regular run to pick up enough "legal" prescription drugs to last him a month.

With all his ploys, still Gordon was strangely ignorant of his own danger. "I stayed with the church some time after my problem began, and eventually everyone but me knew something was wrong," said Gordon. "The addict is always the last one to know. Like all addicts, I labored under two handicaps: delusion and compulsion."

In the pulpit Gordon's demeanor became hyper — talking

too fast, facial muscles twitching, awkward gestures, and sometimes slurred speech. His wife noticed. She would say, "Have you looked in the mirror recently?" and Gordon would respond, "Of course. I look at myself every day." But he couldn't see what others saw.

What others saw wasn't good. From a healthy weight of 180 pounds, Gordon dropped to 126. One woman in the congregation told him outright, "You look like walking death!" But Gordon couldn't understand. The amphetamines made him *feel* healthy and energetic. He thought he could take on the world — until the effect wore off, and he would drop into deep depression.

Finally one Friday morning in November 1967, Gordon looked into the bathroom mirror. He recalls: "I can't tell you why the image had escaped me for so long, but that morning I saw a gaunt, emaciated, ashen-skinned man staring back at me, and I was frightened." He spent the next couple of hours in frantic, bewildered self-recrimination, and then sat down and penned his resignation from Providence Church. He sent the letter to the church with his son and didn't set foot in that church again for fifteen years.

The church had not fired Gordon, a kindness he clings to to this day: "They never did let go of me!" They loved him and prayed for him, asking that he be delivered. But that monkey on his back had a firm grip.

A parishioner arranged a job for Gordon, but within four months it became obvious he couldn't handle it. He spent the next eight months in a private mental hospital for depression. When he left the hospital, he was back in search of his drugs within forty-eight hours.

During the next six years — wandering from town to town, in and out of treatment programs and mental hospitals, spiraling downward — the prince, the pastor of a stellar church, the guy whose "success" most pastors only envy, became a pauper. His church had given him a gracious, beautiful home — not a parsonage but his own home — and he lost it. His marriage broke up. He alienated his children. He could neither find nor hold a steady job.

Gordon took to wandering, removing himself from the reach of all those who loved him and wanted to rescue him. Living on a meager disability check, the pauper took up residence on street corners, park benches, and in rescue missions. Finally mixing alcohol with drugs, Gordon hit bottom. The director of the Charlotte YMCA had to throw him out on the street — Gordon, the erstwhile civic leader — for the drunken disturbance he was causing.

Today, presiding over the recovery center he directs in Charlotte, Gordon once again projects prince-like qualities.

"I wrested myself from the grip of God and wandered for seven years, but I never lost my salvation," Gordon explains. "And something I thought I had lost, I hadn't: my calling. I had blown my ministry sky high. I had divorced, lost my church — I had nothing. I was an addicted, fallen preacher. But a deacon friend visiting me asked, 'Have you forgotten Romans 11:29, that "the gifts and calling of God are without repentance?" ' I was stunned into silence. But it was true.

"It took some doing, but I did return to my calling. And I found when God fixes you back up, he fixes you better than ever before."

So how was Gordon "fixed up"? It happened as suddenly as the downward spiral had been gradual. Gordon was holing up in the facility he now directs, the rescue mission where he occasionally preached as a pastor for the "poor, drunken bums," and he cried out one night in September 1976: "God, either fix me up or take me away!"

He meant it. And God did it. The next morning when Gordon woke up, he headed for the medicine cabinet for the pick-me-up pill he always popped. But for the first time in eleven years, Gordon realized he didn't want one. He hasn't had one since.

It was nothing short of a miracle. There is simply no other explanation for it. Gordon has since been told that the quantities of medication he was taking should have left him a vegetable, if not killed him outright, yet today he is healthy. He should have experienced terrible seizures as he came down from his dependency, yet it never happened.

Gordon received love from many sources. Even during his darkest days, deacons from Providence Baptist sought him out in the mental hospital. Preacher friends found him, even as he tried to hide from them, and they pressed their concern on him. Hundreds of people kept praying.

Now Gordon again meets in executive sessions with the Y director who once tossed him onto the street. He preaches in pulpits across the South. Rebound, the center he now directs, is resurrecting other lives like his. From the depths of a colossal mistake, Gordon has returned to productive and satisfying ministry.

Gordon's story may seem almost too pat: a pastor's mistake tumbles him into dramatic circumstances, he lives through a nightmare, and he recovers from it following a desperate prayer. But Gordon's experience illustrates several points.

First, no one — not even a pastor, not even a successful pastor, a nice person like you or me — escapes mistakes. Failure grabs the spiritual along with the unspiritual.

Second, serious mistakes may begin with small, seemingly innocent decisions. Who would have thought a "harmless" prescription would eventually cost Gordon nearly everything?

Third, Gordon, like many of us, displayed the natural tendency to downplay the danger and ignore warning signs. This mistake on top of his original mistake compounded the mess.

Often pastoral mistakes are more subtle than Gordon's. "What about those mistakes that aren't resolved with a snap of your fingers?" you ask. "I'm not going to become a junkie. My mistakes are more likely to be hiring a mismatch for a staff position or starting an experimental worship service that bombs. How can I recover from these kinds of blunders?"

Mistakes do come in all guises, from garden-variety goofs to mortal sins. The following chapters will examine the rogues' gallery of outright failures and not-so-obvious blunders.

TWO

MAPPING THE TERRITORY

There is the greatest practical benefit in making a few failures early in life.

THOMAS HENRY HUXLEY

The probability of someone watching you is proportional to the stupidity of your actions.

A. KINDSVATER

As a Scout, I took pride in the official Boy Scout compass I hung on a lanyard around my neck. On our trail hikes I would pour over the topographical map of our area, orient myself with compass and landmarks, and then proceed to provide our scoutmaster more running information about the countryside than he probably cared to hear. I learned to pick out the springs, cliffs, creeks, and landmarks that told us where it was safe to hike and camp.

There are probably few things more hazardous than a patrol leader with a map and compass, but I did develop the skill to read the territory. Like most people, I liked knowing where I was going.

Knowing what to avoid also helps. In later years when I led backpacking groups in Yosemite, knowledge of maps and compass helped us steer clear of campsites without water, trails that led nowhere, and unnecessary switchbacks. Most of us prefer not to set out like Lewis and Clark, adventuring into uncharted territory. We like to be familiar with the lay of the land.

Discovering the common potholes and pitfalls of ministry makes sense, too. Although any particular ministerial journey remains largely an unknown, few unique opportunities for mistakes crop up. Other ministers have been in the territory before, sometimes slipping in the mud or falling in the creek, but nonetheless blazing trails. Their experiences can prepare us who follow for the general hazards out there.

Mistakes in Orientation

Beginning the journey on the right trail is crucial. Had I led backpackers north from Tuolumne Meadows, we never would have found our cars in Yosemite Valley. Like guides, pastors want to start out right. But some pastors discover mistakes in orientation have hindered their journey from the beginning.

Greg Ogden, associate pastor at St. John's Presbyterian Church in Los Angeles, tells of his need for reorientation as a rookie assistant pastor in the early seventies:

When I ventured from Southern California to a university ministry in Pittsburgh, I was a ball of fire, ready to explode on the church. Eager to implement the latest (and of course the "right") way to do ministry, I was a cocky twenty-six-year-old who considered the church fortunate to have a ministerial whiz kid set loose in their midst.

I quickly sized up my new boss's approach to ministry as a relic of a bygone era. His early-fifties ministry model taught that the "respected clergy" did the ministry and the congregation played the role of grateful recipient. My thinking, which of course reflected the "biblical model," was that the pastor is to entrust the laity with ministry and work himself out of a job. I was sure the senior pastor was doing it all wrong, which led to a rocky relationship from the start.

The first thing to go was regular pastoral meetings, and I sensed my colleague hardly missed them. My feelings of rejection turned to righteous anger. I thought, *Why should I be the one to pursue him?* But with my critical attitude, I wouldn't have wanted to meet with me, either.

Being fresh out of seminary, I desperately needed affirmation from my boss. When I clashed with the volunteer staff still loyal to my predecessor, I longed to hear the pastor say, "I know it's tough, and I want you to know I'm on your side." But it was not his style to affirm. For him, nothing said was a positive stroke.

The unspoken tension mounted for two years before I decided I could be quiet no more. Seated three feet apart on the overstuffed leather chairs in his office, we faced off.

"For the last two years," I said, "I have wanted to build a relationship with you, but you seemed uninterested." He looked like he wasn't taking it well, but I continued. "You have created an ego-satisfying ministry around yourself, keeping emotionally needy people dependent on you. Nothing can happen in this church unless you are present to give your approval."

As soon as I finished, I wanted to grab my words and stuff them back in my mouth. He retorted, "If you have come to the point where you are questioning my motives in ministry, I do not see how we have any basis for a relationship." Then came the devastating line: " We will no longer relate on a personal level but will stay in touch only to carry out our professional duties." He stood up and showed me to the door.

With my ideal of a shared ministry in shambles, I justified myself by blaming my senior colleague. At my worst moments I wanted his ministry to fail. I quietly delighted in the critical remarks of church members, and sometimes even contributed to their discontent with a pointed word of confirmation.

Besides retribution, my other dominant desire was to flee. But my Jonah-like flight never materialized. It was as if God were taking me by the scruff of my neck and saying, "I'm not letting you leave until I bring the two of you together." That forced me to face the one whom I felt I could justifiably dismiss.

Though it was never spoken, we both were aware of the glaring discrepancy between our rupture and the call on our lives to follow the reconciling Lord. The integrity of the kingdom was at stake. Asking myself, *How did we get here?* I had to own up to my contribution to the rift. I started to see my judgmental spirit and even forced myself to pray for the senior pastor — not asking God to straighten him out but to use him.

Only then did I begin to realize the opportunity I was wasting. Here was a man with twenty years of ministry experience. Though his model was different from mine, he had much to teach me, especially about the compassion my ministry was lacking. As my orientation changed, I began to pick up affirmation from him. He praised me in a sermon; he asked me to accompany him to a conference.

During that six-hour car trip, we actually talked together and related person to person. From that beginning we built a professional relationship. Our ministry approach still differed, but we didn't let it keep us from personal warmth and respect. I think of him now as a man with a compassionate heart who attracts people like a magnet, a man with an active, creative mind and a passion and intensity for Christ.

When the right time came for me to leave and I was packing boxes my last day in the office, there came a knock on the door. In came my boss with the usual Cheshire-cat grin on his face, and he threw open his arms. The hug I got that day contained the joy of reconciliation. Finally, I was ready to begin ministry with a healthy attitude.

For Greg, that attitude made the big difference. A good theory from seminary became a misinterpreted notion, and that notion set him up for the continuing problem that almost terminated his first call. Greg's false start ended favorably, but not until he reoriented himself.

Greg's experience is typical of those making mistakes of orientation. They don't intend to fail, but they chart their future clumsily out of ignorance, inexperience, misconceptions. In such instances a good, long look at the map drawn by other pastors helps avoid some obstacles.

Mistakes of Method

It's hard to build a satisfactory campfire out of the wrong materials. Start with green branches and wet logs, and you end up with a pile of spent matches, smoked coffee, and a cold dinner. In fire building, method means everything.

There are also better and worse ways to go about the business of ministry. Most pastors assume they are doing things right — until their methods fail. Bill Solomon, now pastor of Irmo, South Carolina's Cornerstone Presbyterian Church, recalls his experience with mistaken methods.

"I assumed that because I was the pastor, I knew how to run a church," Bill says with an experienced chuckle. "Was I ever mistaken! I once tried to be a one-man missions committee and run a missions conference solely on sheer enthusiasm. I had absolutely no strategy, and I fell flat on my face. It took a few fiascos like that to realize I had a lot to learn."

Bill recalls another error in practice from his early ministry, this time more serious: "I grew up in a macho atmosphere where we labored under the unspoken assumption that 'women pray, and men get things done.' Praying was fine, but I felt I had to accomplish more tangible things with my time." So Bill slighted his prayer time as a pastor, busying himself with the myriad tasks that consume a pastor's energies.

But such a life becomes exhaustingly broad and dangerously shallow. When personality problems flared within the congregation, Bill tried all the suppression techniques he knew to douse the flames. Nothing worked. "Those nagging problems that wouldn't go away — people on each other's nerves, power plays, hurt feelings — drove me to my knees," he says, "and I saw God perform absolute miracles. He changed minds I considered hopelessly hardened. Personalities aren't supposed to soften like that, but they did.

"I hate to admit it, but only lately have I learned the importance — the value — of prayer. I now give it at least

100 percent more time than I did at the beginning. I count my prayer time now in hours. It was a mistake to slight it in the name of *busyness*."

Bill had not intended wrong. He had simply cast his practice thoughtlessly, and when it hardened into habits, his effectiveness was diminished. It took a crisis for him to reexamine his mold and make needed corrections.

Mistakes of Judgment

Judgment calls constantly burden a backpacking leader. Is this the right fork to take? Can we drink this water? All day long the trail boss makes decisions. Sometimes he or she goofs.

Pastors face similar leadership calls: Should we add a second worship service this fall? Which Sunday school curriculum should we order? What should we do with the inactive members on our roll? Issues, and consequently decisions, arise in a parish as regularly as hunger. And with so many decisions, some will be dillies.

The pastor of a tall-steeple Baptist congregation in a genteel southern community came up with what he considered a fine idea during the Vietnam era. The continuing horror of the war ate at him, and he sought some way to express his concern and that of the church. His idea: to toll the bell in the church tower, calling the community to the peace service he planned. He liked the idea so much he rang the bell himself, standing in the entryway of the grand church and tugging the mournful toll.

It wasn't long before a red-faced deacon stormed up. "You have no right to ring that bell! That's not your bell. It belongs to the church. Now take your hands off it!"

As the deacon stood there with his chest puffed out, the pastor, who had been at the church less than a year, decided discretion was the better part of valor. "I'm sorry," he replied, "I should have cleared my intentions with the deacons. I guess it's not my bell, or anyone else's, and I shouldn't have treated it like my own. Maybe we should talk this over at the next deacons' meeting."

The deacon was barely mollified — he still protested the idea of the service — but the pastor at least kept his pastorate, and his bodily integrity. He came out of that unfortunate decision reminding himself to not overstep his authority.

Another pastor mishandled a runaway phenomenon in the church by doing nothing. He was senior pastor of a staid old church full of money, manners, and momentum. Not much swayed the congregation from its historic course — until the faithful evangelistic callers, tired of ineffectiveness, prayed for greater spiritual power. They got it — in abundance.

This handful of leaders became excited about their new-found spiritual gifts. Speaking in tongues and beginning to reach out to others, they soon had some of the more tradition-bound members on edge. When the enthusiastic group began inviting charismatic speakers, and others from outside the church began flocking to special meetings, it was too much for the traditional element. "They're trying to take the church away from us!" became the most common complaint.

While church members were choosing sides in escalating skirmishes, the pastor took the attitude that the whole thing would blow over, and continued on as if he were still pastoring a sleeping giant. Frequently out of town speaking or leading tours, he was absent at exactly the time he needed to exercise a strong hand.

He allowed the problem to boil to such intensity that the denomination was twice called in: once to "fix the charismatic problem," and when that didn't do what some wanted, a second time to remove the pastor. He was not removed, but the commission declared his actions "not prudent" and invited the disgruntled members to leave.

Many did leave, severely affecting the viability of the congregation. Shortly thereafter the pastor left, retiring early. The situation might have resolved itself under other circumstances, but not this time. The pastor made a bad call, and by misjudging the severity of the discord, he brought his ministry to a premature and discouraging finish.

He was more fortunate in misjudgment than Union Major General John Sedgwick. At the Civil War Battle of Spotsylvania, Sedgwick insisted on standing up and looking over the parapet. When his officers cautioned him to keep down, he replied, "Nonsense! They couldn't hit an elephant at this dist—"

Mistakes of judgment can be deadly, even if figuratively. Sometimes pastors make great calls and everybody cheers. Other times their best judgment is deficient, and the fans are ready to "throw the bum out." It's enough to make most church leaders cautious.

Mistakes with People

Mistakes of orientation, method, and judgment provide their share of danger, but the territory becomes particularly perilous on the interpersonal frontier. There emotions set tricky hazards, and these hazards clustered around interpersonal mistakes often rip the biggest holes in the pastor's seamless garment.

Forget to take the offering some Sunday — an institutional gaffe — and people kid you for weeks. But neglect calling on Ernest Selfworthy's aged mother — an interpersonal faux pas — and they begin to warm the tar. Many pastors will tell you their most painful mistakes were interpersonal — with parishioners, staff members, or their own families.

Mistakes with parishioners. I once heard a pastor quip about his difficult charge: "This would be a great church if it weren't for the people." Church members are hard to map. They don't stand still like mountains. You can't depend on them like a well-marked trail. Sometimes they seem to delight in devilry and persist in perniciousness. Yet they are also completely capable of coming through when you least expect them, blessing the church in spite of themselves. Their unpredictability offers ample opportunity for church leaders to err — leaders who are themselves members of the rascally race.

Dale Street, the new pastor of a church that had been served for over twenty years by its organizing pastor, found himself in a Catch-22. The beloved founding pastor had resigned suddenly and rather mysteriously. However, he left his mark on the congregation. Some of his final sermons railed against "wolves out to pervert the doctrinal purity of the church," and mentioned a certain seminary.

That seminary just happened to be Dale's alma mater. And the pastor didn't want Dale to be his successor. So although he was unsuccessful in discouraging the search committee from calling Dale, he left Dale in a precarious position. People were set to scrutinize Dale's every word from the pulpit.

Dale enjoyed eight months of honeymoon before trouble surfaced. A small handful of members began applying heat to this pastor who was "soft on inerrancy." They circulated an inflammatory flier. They took elders to lunch. They spoke out in meetings. And Dale began to reel from the impact of this opposition.

Finally a meeting was called for two of the chief antagonists to air their concerns with the elders. Their major complaint: "Dale does not believe in biblical inerrancy."

Dale's flabbergasted response: "But I *do* believe in inerrancy. I've said it publically and signed without reservation the church doctrinal statement. What's more, I demonstrate it in the way I preach and teach the Word of God."

The detractors were undeterred. "You see, what we have here is a man who says he believes in inerrancy, who will even sign a statement saying he believes it, but who in his heart of hearts really doesn't believe it. How can a man like that be our pastor?"

So Dale was stuck. Signing the statement "proved" he was a liar. Not signing it would substantiate his unbelief. He couldn't win with that suspicious knot of parishioners.

Dale had made no mistakes to bring him to this point, however, and he avoided them as he worked his way out of the dilemma. Fortunately, the great majority of the congregation and its leadership did not buy the paradoxical reasoning of the disgruntled group. A small band did eventually leave the church, but Dale was spared to continue ministering effectively in a situation that eventually stabilized.

Dale's greatest task was to restrain himself from assuming the attack mode. A sermon he had written to devastate the opposition remained crumpled in his wastebasket while he preached on brotherhood. He thumbtacked a card he'd hand-lettered — TRUTH WILL TRIUMPH — to the pulpit to restrain his desire to lash out. Dale reacted with warmth and care — at considerable personal expense — and most of the people followed his lead.

Although Dale avoided interpersonal mistakes for the most part, there is a limit to how much we can control interpersonal relationships. Somebody will always be edgy about something. Mark Erickson, pastor of Eastbrook Church in Milwaukee, is also a physician specializing in emergency medicine. He enjoys telling this story:

"One day when I was in the emergency room, we received word that an elderly lady was being rushed to us after collapsing in a Catholic church. When she arrived, the medics bringing her in were thumping on her chest, working feverishly. We immediately defibrillated her and started all sorts of IVs — doing all we could to help this poor woman.

"Finally she woke up and looked around rather startled. Then she got mad. 'Oh no!' she lamented. 'This is the *third* time this has happened. I keep expecting to wake up in heaven!' She was terribly disappointed, and she was angry at us for doing what we did to save her. Sometimes you just can't win with people, so it helps if we don't take ourselves too seriously."

Mistakes with staff. For some reason, the church office is particularly hazardous territory. Perhaps it's the clash of worldly ambition and heavenly zeal, or the echo of competing egos. At any rate, mistakes with staff have riven many a church.

Pastors who manage a volunteer or professional staff shoulder a number of interpersonal responsibilities: delegating work fairly, providing spiritual counsel, maintaining lines of communication and accountability, giving opportunity for growth, sharing the spoils of success and the blame for failure. All provide convenient opportunities for error. But mistakes in calling and dismissing staff often seem the most harmful.

An Assemblies of God pastor put his finger on one mistake in hiring: "I've made my commitments too early. As a pastor, I'm accustomed to looking for the best in people, so I tend to 'fall in love' with candidates. I focus on their good points and gloss over their shortcomings. It's those bad habits, their poor track records, that return to haunt me.

"When I interviewed one applicant we later hired, I mistook ego for confidence. That staff member's inflated self-importance became a continual problem. Every time he was in front of people, the attention had to be on him. It got to the point where people were pulling me aside and saying, 'I don't want to sound mean, but we've got to get rid of him. He's ruining every program he's involved in.'

"I had to admit I had made a mistake. I had imagined flowers in what we now could see was a weed patch. We finally eased him off the staff, and I have since developed a healthy skepticism. I'm looking for a servant's heart, so an overactive ego is a red light."

Another pastor said, "I want to believe people, especially those who want to serve the Lord in Christian ministries. So I feel awkward checking their references. But I'm never again going to hire an associate without talking with previous supervisors. We've been burned too many times."

Mistakes in hiring inevitably lead to that second great opportunity for error: the process of terminating an employee. Although there is no easy way to fire a staff member, there are many inept ways to do it.

One pastor ruefully recalls, "I had a youth director who had a hard time keeping his hands off the gals in his group. It was nothing grossly obvious, yet I kept hearing complaints. Three or four times I called him into my office and confronted him. Each time, with a mixture of shock and chagrin, he assured me that everything would be okay; he'd curtail any activities that would give even 'the appearance of evil.'

"Then, a few weeks or months later, I'd get another complaint. The guy had a moral problem. Out of misguided charity or simple naiveté — whatever — I waited too long to fire him. Finally I called him in and told him he'd have to resign. We gave him a thousand dollars and moving expenses. He left without a word.

"I was lucky things worked out as well as they did. It's a grave error to fire too late."

Acting without board approval, retaining the guilty party too long after giving notice, giving a rosy but inaccurate recommendation for a fired employee, and mishandling the announcement of a staff member's "resignation" are other ways pastors have dropped the ball in firing staff. It's a rocky path to termination, full of well-intentioned yet costly mistakes.

Mistakes with loved ones. Of all the mistakes that tear at a pastor's psyche, failures at home are the worst. Other pastors can debrief the disastrous board meeting or commiserate over a blunder before the bedtable light is switched off. But the pastor whose tragic mistake *is* his home life has only a dark bedroom or a domestic battlefield to return to at night. A rattled family shakes every other aspect of life.

Rookie cops are warned of the three worst hazards of the profession, and they are not bullets, bludgeons, and Bowie knives. Problems with alcohol, money, and women have cashiered more peace officers than any violent means. From at least the time of Paul, rookie preachers have been warned, too, to keep their personal and familial lives in order.

Yet sometimes the ministry seems almost to work against that. One pastor, who now is again enjoying fulfilling ministry, relates his story:

"My problem came from the need to achieve. I had to accomplish everything by thirty-five so I could be ahead of the others who wanted it all by forty. I published umpteen books, served on the board of a major university, got my name in *Who's Who in America*, and accumulated all kinds of honors. But it exacted a toll on my marriage.

"When my marriage got really bad, I felt I couldn't remain in my parish, so I took on the directorship of a public agency. It was better to be out of the ministry while we were going through all the pain and mess of trying to straighten out our lives. After a lot of counseling, we eventually decided to go our separate ways, and that was so painful. It felt like I had lost everything I once held dear.

"As I can see it now, my divorce resulted from my inability to integrate the emotional and the professional. Being a super-achiever in one area depleted me in the other. I was a young hard charger, out of touch with my emotions because I'd been on an intellectual, activist trip."

In the midst of stellar accomplishments as a pastor, this man's failure as a husband destroyed his marriage and nearly undid his ministry. That was a steep bill to foot for a ministry mistake. The price is always high when it comes to family.

Both impersonal and interpersonal hazards dot the ministry map, and at times they make the going difficult, even perilous. Yet often these gross mistakes appear almost easy to avoid compared to the tricky "little" mistakes lurking in the underbrush.

THREE

THE INSIDIOUS MISTAKE

A small error in the beginning is a great one in the end.

THOMAS AQUINAS

Perhaps you have read this far with a sense of relief: no drug problem, your initial pastorate went smoothly, nobody yet has tried to take your scalp, you get along with your co-workers, and the family appears content, even if they do grumble some now and then.

Maybe mistakes are for other, less fortunate, leaders. You've scanned the horizon without sighting any torpedoes.

Beware the barnacles!

Most of us aren't spectacular in our error. For every sudden fiery wreck exist numerous slow sinkings brought on by years of negligent maintenance. A popular Christian writer divorces, and people everywhere register shock. Twenty drained pastors quietly resign, and it is hardly noticed. Yet in either case, the damage is considerable.

Or a minister pockets part of the offering — and creates a stir. But many other ministers slowly deplete their spiritual substance — and cause a wider loss. The insidious mistakes can sink us almost imperceptibly, but sunk is sunk.

So what are these chronic little mistakes, the overlooked systemic errors that bring more than their share of grief? Most anything in immoderate quantities will do the trick. For instance, pastoral calling is a time-honored duty; yet do *only* pastoral calling, and people get upset.

Tagging all the dangerous little mistakes is impossible, but listing a few common ones will make the point.

Goatfeathers

A sensitive Reformed pastor provided this colorful tag for a common behavior: "It seems we pastors are often out collecting 'goatfeathers' for our cap. By *goatfeathers* I mean those pats on the back for the favors we do. Somebody asks me to pray for Rotary, and I do it. I know I'll be awarded a couple of goatfeathers for the effort, and I kind of like the approval.

"The problem is, collecting goatfeathers takes me away from my real ministry. I easily can get so involved in my collection that I miss the essence of what God called me to do. I'm not in the ministry to grant favors and collect approval, but those very activities can subtly distract me from the essential tasks of ministry like teaching and preaching and caring for people."

Goatfeathers are awarded for many activities, most of which are honorable enough in themselves. It's just that they can consume a ministry. One pastor found himself taking a woman to the doctor's office several times a month over a period of years. It was a caring thing to do. It showed pastoral concern. But this and similar activities took so much time that his administration of the church fell into shambles and his sermons started sounding like he composed them on the spot — which he sometimes did.

Some pastors, finding little satisfaction in a local parish, harvest goatfeathers farther up the denominational ladder. One middle-aged pastor of a dead-in-the-water church feathered his cap with district responsibilities. Mainly by the volume of time he spent at the district level, this pastor eventually found himself chairman of the regional policy board. He had clout. He had a title. He had a gavel.

He also had a church still struggling to remain viable, struggling now without benefit of the time or interest of its pastor. He could make most of the district meetings, no matter where they were, because he preferred traveling to them over calling at the hospital. He spent far more effort preparing opening remarks or press releases for the district than he did preparing his weekly sermon.

Many pastors have found the little mistake of pursuing goatfeathers leaves themselves short for the truly important matters. And that lessens their value. When someone asked Mark Twain how he would feel about being ridden out of town on a rail, he replied, "If it weren't for the honor of it, I'd just as soon walk." Goatfeathers carry little esteem when attached to the body with tar.

Tangents

It's easy to lose track of what business we're in. An English newspaper reported in 1976 that certain buses no longer stopped for passengers on the Hanley to Bagnall route. The official reason made transportation history: If these buses stopped to pick up passengers, it would throw off the timetable!

Tangents plague ministry, too. "I've got to keep myself from going off on tangents," one pastor confided. "I can easily become so concerned about some cause that I'm apt to redefine the gospel around it."

Theoretically, a ministry can be centered on any number of things. In some churches, fellowship is supreme; in others, a teaching ministry. One pastor will shepherd her congregation with evangelism as the guiding principle; another will mold his congregation around serving a deteriorating neighborhood.

The question is not so much *which* activity will be the rallying point (as long as it is an honorable undertaking for a church), but *is it appropriate* to the congregation? Churches will rally around any one of many different flags. It is a mistake, however, to wave too many, or ill-chosen, flags.

"In Pittsburgh in the sixties, I stood up for the blacks,"

our tangent-prone pastor continued. "It was an honorable thing to do, but I put the heat to my people too quickly. If they weren't ready to agree with me, I was about ready to read them out of the kingdom.

"Civil rights, as good a cause as it was, angled us away from the heart of our ministry. If I make anything other than Christ the center of my ministry, I'm not sticking to my gospel work."

The Evil One delights in perverting a good activity. If he can get us to chase butterflies — even majestic ones — instead of following the Dove, he would be pleased. The little mistake of choosing the wrong center, or too many centers, keeps much essential work from being accomplished.

Stunted Growth

Another insidious mistake especially plagues over-booked pastors.

The dossier told of fifteen years of pastoral experience. The frank reference painted a different picture: "Although Scott has been ordained for fifteen years, it appears to me that he has had three years of experience five times over. I have witnessed no growth."

Scott was not much of a student. He did okay in college and squeaked through seminary. Leaving the commencement proceedings, Scott whooped, tossed his mortarboard in the air, and proclaimed: "Free at last! I never want to see another book."

He was called to a small church in rural Montana and immersed himself in ministry. In two and a half years he moved to another church. Three years later he moved again. He stayed four years at a third, one and a half at another, and was four years at his fifth church in fifteen years. Now he is looking again.

The problem? "I start out great," Scott says, "but about two years into a pastorate I begin to wonder, *What do I have left to say?* By that point I have used up the sermons I wrote in

Bible college and seminary. I've covered the basic points of doctrine. So I get restless." No church has asked Scott to leave; they like his warm spirit and easy way with people. He just gets antsy about every three years. He's suffering from stunted growth.

In Scott's busy schedule of people concerns, administration, and personal fitness, he has carved no niche for study. He seldom reads. He doesn't listen to other preachers. He takes no magazines or journals. There's no continuing education program that interests him.

Nothing feeds his springs of creativity. He has to rely on his limited supply, and when that runs out, he's off to a new spot where he's again a novelty.

Scott is now getting bored with his life as a pastor. "I've thought about becoming a lawyer," he confides, "but does the world need any more lawyers? And besides, it would involve three more years of school and the bar exams. I couldn't take that. I just wish I found ministry a little more exciting. Maybe the next church will be more stimulating."

It probably won't. Scott has made the little mistake of forgetting one precious element in the pastor's schedule: personal growth and enrichment. Ministerial midgets think small, preach small, and live small because of this small mistake.

Unreliability

For nearly five of his eight years in a small Oregon town, local seniority made Don the dean of clergy in town — all five of them. Since other pastors were arriving and departing with the regularity of a commuter train, he was considered president of the ministerial association by default.

Most of the time he considered the pastoral fellowship a lifesaver. The majority of his fellow pastors were nice enough, but some he found annoyingly unreliable in keeping commitments. "I'll take the benediction for the sunrise service," one would promise, but when Easter arrived, the supposedly willing participant would be a no-show.

"Then it's agreed. We'll jointly sponsor that musical," the group decided. *Celebrate Life!* came and went with scant attendance and a bundle of bills for Don's church to cover. Then he'd hear, "We decided to have our retreat that weekend. By the way, how'd that revival go?"

"It was a Christian musical."

"Yeah, that's right. How'd we do, anyway?"

The "flake factor" worried Don. He often wondered if the fellow who never wrote down the next meeting but always said, "Now you be sure to call me!" missed as many of his other appointments. Did the one who committed himself for every baccalaureate service and never came do the same with weddings and funerals? *How can he build solid ministry on unreliability?* Don wondered. Then he looked at the fellow's work and he understood: he didn't.

Forgetfulness, irresponsibility, or downright dodging commitments usually come in small doses. No one occurrence is all that damning, but the cumulative effect of each small mistake leaves the scent of unreliability across one's whole ministry.

Workaholism

I once knew a woman who was convinced that ministers were "no-account sponges." As she was growing up, her parents entertained countless itinerant preachers. She'd watch them show up at mealtime — sometimes uninvited — and thin the servings of fried chicken. *Why don't they work for a living?* she wondered. *Then they wouldn't have to eat other people's food.*

Admittedly, not all her models were prime specimens, but I would beg to differ with her. The pastors I run across, if anything, edge toward workaholic practices. Their high calling and the never-ending nature of their profession tend to produce too taxing a schedule. And who was ever acclaimed for *moderating* ministry expectations? The strokes go to those who practically (and sometimes literally) kill themselves.

One pastor's confession: "I worked seven days a week for years. Mornings, holidays, late at night — I'd be at it. I had a messiah complex: If I don't do it, it won't be done right. But I hurt my family. That's where the rub comes. You can't be absent all the time and expect your family not to feel the pain." For this pastor it necessitated a long, slow process of change. He feels fortunate; it didn't take a total disintegration of his family to trigger his change. He caught the distress signals before his ship went down.

Marilee Pierce Dunker's *Man of Vision, Woman of Prayer* sheds light on the terrible price she, her mother, and her siblings paid for the indefatigable ministry of her father, Bob Pierce, founder of World Vision International. Pierce would not be hindered in his compassionate crusade for the needy of the world. Hundreds of thousands were literally saved from death, in part by his work. Yet his single-minded zeal cost Pierce. A daughter committed suicide. His praying wife separated from him. The rest of his alienated family were reconciled to him only hours before his death.

Bob Pierce really did do much for so many. How could devotion to his calling be a mistake? His "little" mistake was pushing himself beyond his own capacity. He could not be all things to all people. It may have been intemperate to try, but it wasn't hard.

Workaholism at first gives out the wrong signals. Life's reinforcements appear set up to instill the workaholic nature. Success, acclaim, and results come from hard work, and the more you work, the greater the return — for a while. Only later does the law of diminishing returns set in.

This economic law states that although greater investment usually brings greater returns, at some point the ratio of returns to investment begins to diminish; the harder you work, the *less* you get in return. Knowing the point where the law kicks in is the essence of economic planning — and the key to wise stewardship of one's time and energy.

A pastor in Los Angeles took a worn-out church, and

through love and superhuman efforts turned it into a show-case congregation. He followed several pastors who had either shocked, neglected, or abused the congregation. The folks in that church had seen it all, and been turned off.

This new pastor showed them they hadn't seen it all; a good church could be exciting. With incautious disregard for his own physical limitations, he determinedly nursed the church back to health.

Eventually the church was doing fine, but *he* was nearly gone. In the midst of his success, this enormously talented and deeply committed pastor entered a deep depression. He came within a hair's breadth of taking his own life. He learned he absolutely could not continue taxing his body as he had done, and his body had simply shut down and pulled him into the depression until he conceded.

Workaholism cheats not only one's family; it puts one's body into a deficit economy, and only a government can sustain that kind of "small" mistake.

Sticky Involvements

Sometimes projects begin well but digress from that point. Roger Carpenter, a Methodist pastor, experienced such a problem.

"My wife got involved in selling home-care products in our community — soap and things like that," Roger said. "She wanted to put aside some money for our kid's college years, and besides, it gave her a creative outlet. As her sales picked up, she asked me to help. I wasn't too excited about an outside business proposition, but I decided to join her for something to do together — to give her my support. Well, I got pulled in hook, line, and sinker.

"Before long we were inviting friends and church members over for sales presentations. I tried to keep this aspect of my life separate from my identity as pastor of the church, but it was impossible. Soon I started being seen as 'the pastor who hustles soap.' It compromised my witness in the community, and all the time I was becoming more and more embarrassed by it. I should never have allowed myself to spoil my witness."

Not everybody would censure Roger. Had he broken any laws? Deceived anybody? Bent any commandments? No. Had he misused church time and pastoral influence? Maybe a little. However, Roger felt he had compromised his station, succumbed to the route of least resistance. He was so embarrassed by his involvement in the sales scheme that he welcomed a call to a new community where he would not be known as the compromised preacher.

The insidious mistake traps its prey like the proverbial frog who boiled to death in a pot warmed slowly. Degree by degree, instance by instance, the chronic mistakes work their evil. Rarely spectacular in their course, they nonetheless become deadly in their metastasis.

FOUR

MORAL FAILURES

When I err, everyone can see it, but not when I lie.

JOHANN WOLFGANG VON GOETHE

Man-like it is to fall into sin,
Fiend-like it is to dwell therein;
Christ-like it is for sin to grieve,
God-like it is all sin to leave.

FRIEDRICH VON LOGAU

While some mistakes have FOOL-ISH or UNFORTUNATE stamped across them, others have FORBIDDEN. Showing up Thursday for Wednesday's appointment is not too swift; showing up in Switzerland with the church treasury is sin. Both are mistakes, but the difference is qualitative as well as quantitative. The added moral dimension puts sin in a completely different category from blunders.

Generally, church leaders are held in high esteem as persons who believe in something — something measured by canons of right and wrong. The general public, church members, and, for that matter, the leaders themselves, expect not only intellectual assent but behavioral adherence to the belief system. So for an acknowledged leader to make a moral error is to live a lie. When a pastor or other prominent Christian falls, the shock waves fan out in all directions, weakening the foundations of churches everywhere. Amazement and shock over sinful conduct disrupt a church far more than incredulity over a poor decision.

Moreover, to opt for the wrong is more than an unfortunate choice, a stupid venture, a silly slip; it's an offense against the glory of God. More than pragmatic considerations come into play. When our Sovereign is offended, the first question needs to be "What must I do to be saved?" rather than "How can I prevent this from dashing my plans?"

Of all the mistakes, living a lie carries the greatest consequences, for the ripples extend beyond This Age to the Age to Come.

Moses transported from Mount Sinai a list of ten such mistakes, and many more arise from the pages of Scripture. The territory is marked OFF LIMITS on the map, but some pastors find their way into this forbidden country.

A Costly Charade

The pulpit of Christ Church in picturesque Carmel is one of those ecclesiastical plums; it rates among the top five in California.

Carmel-by-the-Sea speaks of tasteful aristocracy. Apart from claiming a movie star as mayor, the city fills its expensive hostelries in a decent, quiet manner befitting the old wealth that inhabits the town. It's on the beach, but a proper beach more accustomed to sweaters than string bikinis. Carmel is a sheltered haven of respectability, and Christ Church is one of its most prominent and respected institutions.

Only one church in Carmel predates Christ Church. The Carmel Mission was founded in 1771 by Father Junipero Serra, that tenacious church planter who sewed together California with a string of missions. But Christ Church came on its heels to gather the Protestant faithful of this historic community, and a string of the brightest and sharpest pastors in the region led Christ Church to prominence among churches.

To this church in 1965 came Robert Millen. He was thirty-eight, younger than most of his predecessors, but his credentials fit the position. In thirteen years as a pastor (plus a few odd years as a student pastor), Robert had taken four struggling churches and left them robust powerhouses a few years later. Every one of them remained strong and effective after he left, a testimony to skill that matched his outstanding personality. The marriage of Robert Millen and Christ Church appeared made in heaven.

Robert's situation was enviable. The manse, a red-tiled hacienda, overlooks the Pacific Ocean through twisted cypress trees. Membership in a Carmel Valley country club fattened his ample salary package. Robert especially enjoyed lunching there among the movers and shakers of Carmel society, and the church expected it. In fact, the congregation graciously shared him outside the church, allowing him great freedom to speak at ministers' conferences and denominational activities. None of this Robert took for granted. He worked hard to pastor his generous congregation.

For nearly ten years, Robert led Christ Church with all the expertise and dedication anyone could ask. Always a strong, biblically sound preacher, he pleasantly surprised the board with his administrative skills, the congregation with his pastoral concern, and the denomination with his willing leadership. If you lived on the West Coast, you probably knew of Robert; and if you knew him, you spoke highly of him. Robert was that kind of guy.

Robert was also bisexual. He'd known it, struggled with it, and ached over his capitulation to it for two decades.

Being bright and resourceful, Robert had managed masterfully to hide his festering sin. No one knew — not his church, not his denominational superiors, not his friends in the community, and certainly not his wife. Robert pursued his life with such characteristic skill, they probably never would have known had not the inner burden become unbearable.

"I played everything else in life completely above board," Robert explains. "I was Mr. Straight Arrow — except for this. I'm not a hiding kind of person, so it killed me bit by bit to live a lie.

"I knew homosexual practice was sinful. Try as I could, I couldn't stretch the Bible enough to make it okay. I can't tell you how many times I vowed to myself never again to do it, but as many times as I vowed, I eventually caved in.

"Can you imagine, living in one world as the upright, successful, 'moral' leader of a community, and in another world as a driven captive of desire? I'd preach, but inside I could only condemn myself: *You corrupt impostor! Who are you to preach anything? You're the worst kind of hypocrite.* And my unending success made it worse. For twenty years, I was expecting God to strike me down — I'd even pray for it — but in return, everything I did prospered. The contrast between who I was and what I accomplished never ceased to dismay me. When I'd see real saints laboring without any of the rewards I received, it always got to me."

When the pent-up pressure became too great, Robert subconsciously blew his cover. His daughter had been in a serious accident, and her hospitalization and eventual death added stress to the family. In what Robert considers "a really stupid way," he let slip a clue: he left a note from a companion on the dresser. His wife found it and confronted Robert.

For a while, Robert thought they might patch things up. But the humiliation and especially the history of twenty years of deceit proved too reprehensible to his wife. Soon after they buried their daughter, Robert's wife and son moved out in vindictive rage.

Years of hiding, years of battling a vicious enemy and losing, years of living a lie, and then the loss of his family nearly drove Robert over the brink. He considered walking into the Pacific surf and swimming out to sea. An end to life sounded better than the shambles of his exposed life. But he was sharp enough to commit himself to a psychiatric hospital instead.

One week after entering the hospital, Robert Millen sent a letter to Christ Church, resigning his pastorate. With that letter he relinquished his good name, his lunches at the club, his adobe mansion, his oak pulpit, his livelihood, and most of his future. But the letter had character. Robert spelled out his moral failing with delicate clarity. He confessed. He made no excuses; he requested no favors. He asked only for their prayers and their forgiveness for his sin, fully expecting awkward silence at best and more likely hostile reprisals. He knew how *he* felt about himself, and he expected them to feel the same. Yet he received from his congregation amazingly open and warm forgiveness, even as they did what they had to do: accept his resignation.

"If you hadn't walked around in our lives, we would have been less blessed," they told him. When he left the hospital nearly seven weeks later, the outpouring of love startled him. With literally nothing — his wife had taken all their family belongings — he had to rely on the charity of his friends, a bitter realization for a man accustomed to making his own way. But somebody loaned him a car, and somebody else arranged a place for him to live. Months later he found a position in Oregon as manager of a group-care facility for the elderly. He learned the ropes quickly, and survived.

The pastor of the church he ended up attending in Oregon knew Robert's past. He also knew Robert, so he urged him to teach a seniors' class. Robert enjoyed the opportunity to minister, and it kept him thinking about positive things.

Robert has maintained celibacy for some time now. He says it's not easy. It probably never will be. But it beats living a lie.

Sin, although a tragic mistake, is so much more than a mistake. Robert could not just grin sheepishly, say "I goofed," and get on with ministry. His brand of mistake — moral failing — ushered in drastic consequences: loss, a constant battle with himself, life that will never again be the same.

The story would probably have had many of the same elements had he injured a deacon in a rage, run off with his secretary, been proved a fraud, or siphoned church money into his own account. Immorality, lying, cheating, stealing, or injuring others bear consequences far greater than those of mere blunders or even major mistakes.

The leaders of God's people are expected to match proclamation with practice. When their lives are exposed as a living contradiction of their message, all hell laughs.

And yet we all sin. Ministers make mistakes, little or large, innocent or culpable, sooner or later. Since we are bound to make them, probably in many varieties, how best can we manage them? Or, better yet, how can we even *benefit* from mistakes? That is our remaining topic.

FIVE

FACING THE FAILURE

Who errs and mends, to God himself commends.

MIGUEL DE CERVANTES SAAVEDRA

A rooster's crow pierced the heart of the frightened and derelict disciple. One glance at the Master's expression, and all Peter could do was weep bitterly.

Yet Peter is not remembered as a man of tears and failure. Certainly he filled his quota of mistakes. Previously, his brief trek on the water turned into treading water, and later Paul would rebuke him publicly for his snub of the Hellenistic Christians. Still Peter stands in our minds as the rock — a venerated founder of the church.

Why? Because Peter learned to face failure. Failure wasn't the end for Peter; it was merely one milestone. Other more significant monuments marked the greater course of his life, overshadowing the lesser markers of mistakes. He who tried big, blundered big, but he continued on. And we are all blessed because of it.

Biting the Bullet

Richard Kew, an Episcopal rector, discovered that failure wears a dread countenance. A couple of years ago he wrote autobiographically:

"Last week I resigned from parish ministry. My marriage is in trouble and my nerves have been in tatters. Less than a year ago I was considered a high flyer in my denomination, having held a series of highly responsible positions of leadership by the time I was in my mid-thirties.

"Now all that is gone. I have burned out. The succession of emotions I have experienced over the last couple of years has been devastating — depression, despair, disgust, anguish, panic, sadness — and all the time it has been increasingly impossible to put one foot in front of the other. Every time I stood in the pulpit or at the Communion table, I felt myself digging for spiritual and emotional resources that no longer were there. Like a thirsty man, week by week I would go to a dry well, hoping for a small puddle of water seeping in from somewhere."

His attitude toward Sunday worship was the clue he failed to notice. "For as long as I can remember, I have dreaded Sundays. They became the symbol of the agony I was having with my work. People came because they wanted to hear what I had to say from God. I wanted to tell them, 'I have nothing to give you; now it is your turn to feed me,' but I didn't."

Preaching, which had once been his great delight, slowly became a nightmare, until he reached the point where he stood at the pulpit one Sunday thinking, *I don't believe a word I'm saying.* Soon afterward, he found himself wondering whether God existed at all. *Certainly if he does,* he thought, *he doesn't appear too interested in me.*

"Instead of correctly interpreting the danger signs, I kept on going. In order to stay where I was and to appear on top of things, I found myself pushing harder and harder. In due course, everything caught up with me, in the most excruciating manner. I discovered I was not on top of anything; everything was on top of me. By the time I started taking action to redeem the situation, my problems were already too big to be resolved."

The problem? He continually overspent his emotional ac-

count. "I always felt myself to be stronger and more capable than I actually was," Kew writes, "and I also wanted to prove something to myself, my peers, and the whole wide world. I deliberately took on tough assignments, and by and large succeeded.

"Prospective secular employers, after reading my résumé, have looked over their half-moon glasses and wondered how I found time to do it all. The answer: I stole the time from my family and myself."

His creeping acedia, the hurry-up pace, the dread accompanying his work, his loss of confidence in the Master and message he represented — all should have put the brakes on his frenetic scramble before the eventual collapse of his marriage and career. Clearly something was amiss, but he continued to ignore the signals. Only when blaring sirens drowned out all else did he slow down to assess the situation. By then he had a first-class disaster on his hands.

The result? "By the time my wife and I sat down in marriage counseling, the backlog of unfinished business was too great. Tension had mounted to the point we decided we could not live under the same roof. I resigned my pastorate, moved into a rented room, and tried to put my life back together. There was not only the deep sense of failure my wife and I shared — along with mutual recrimination — but the church I served for a number of years became a source of anguished upset as they probed clumsily to place blame for the fiasco."

Kew found himself without his occupation, his identity, his family, his possessions, his home, and — nearly — his faith. "I had been unable to say no," he laments, "hungry for recognition and too eager to prove myself more capable than anyone else. We cannot reach beyond ourselves, but I spent years trying to do just that. The success was transitory, the fall devastating."

Fortunately Kew didn't remain in a hole, and he is now director of the U.S. office of The Society for Promoting Christian Knowledge. But his words pierce us when we're apt to ignore the signs of an impending mistake: "I hope clergy will

see the danger signs and realize when they are running out of steam. I was too stubborn to do anything about it at first. If this is you, too, then I urge you, for God's sake and for the sake of those around you, to *do* something about it before it is too late. Parish ministry can be a killer, and a dead or neutralized pastor is no good to anybody."

Where does recovery begin? As difficult as it seems to the one feverishly trying to stonewall his failings, the first step toward recovery is admitting the problem: "I have *failed*." Kew couldn't begin to conquer the failure-beast until he named it. To begin to recover, he, like all of us, needed to recognize his mistakes.

Recognizing Failure

In *Where Is God When It Hurts?* Philip Yancey wrote about a peculiar handicap of lepers: they feel no pain in the afflicted parts of their body. They can burn a leprous hand in the fire or have a toe gnawed off by a rat, and never feel a thing. A cut becomes abcessed or an injury critical because they have no sensation of pain. Much of the disfigurement of leprosy comes not from the disease but from the tragic side effect of painlessness. Pain, then, is a blessing.

One of the marks of a sociopathic personality is an inability to recognize one's own error. The sociopath can lie, swindle, and abuse, and never really understand why everybody gets so worked up about it. Like the leper, bereft of the merciful capacity to feel pain, the sociopath injures himself and others and totally ignores it. He makes mistakes and goes on as if nothing happened.

Minor errors, when unattended, soon become gross infractions. Thus, the dawning pain of failure is, for those sensitive enough to experience it, a blessed protection. We should be glad we feel bad when we fail. It's a vital safeguard for the healthy — one from which the sociopath never benefits.

What we do with that signal is another matter. Richard Kew at first ignored the pain and pressed on. What he needed to do

was stop to recognize the source of that pain. Only then could he possibly have avoided turning his world inside out.

Claiming the Failure

Harold Englund of Garden Grove Community Church quips, "When I lay an egg, I autograph it and hold it up for all to see." That's not bad advice, for it accomplishes two objectives in one stroke.

First, it keeps him from waffling. How much more constructive to say "I've blown it!" than to hem and haw and cover his tracks. Admitting failure begins the healing process, a process that cannot commence during mental gymnastics to avoid the blame.

Earl Palmer of First Presbyterian Church in Berkeley, California, tells an anecdote about Karl Barth: "When Barth went back to Germany after World War II, he met theologian after theologian who said, 'We have been through a demonic period with Adolf Hitler.' Even non-Christians were saying, 'What we've experienced was demonic.' Everyone claimed, in effect, 'The Devil was responsible.' Barth said he yearned to hear someone say, 'We sinned.' He felt there wouldn't be help until they could admit their own culpability."

Had Richard Kew placed the blame outside himself, he would have delayed his recovery. Autographing that egg, claiming it as his own, was the initial hard but necessary step toward his recovery.

Second, holding it up for all to see is a masterful strategy. I don't think I am alone in my great fear of mistakes: I don't want to be discovered. Quiet little mistakes that nobody sees don't terrorize my imagination like public blunders that can leave me dangling in the breeze. *I urged them to increase the budget, and now we're swimming in red ink. How soon till the inquisition?* Or *That new roof was my idea, but it leaks like a sieve. That's going to come back to haunt me!* The apprehension of being caught, getting stuck with the rap, is sometimes worse than the actual experience.

We disarm the opponent when we expose our own folly. One of the secrets of judo is to use the momentum of the attacker. You don't block the punch; you go with it. It works with confessions as well. "Friends, I goofed. Last fall I urged you to increase the budget 35 percent against all signs to the contrary. I felt we could be stretched. We couldn't. Now we have some hard decisions to make, and it's my fault. What can I say? I was wrong."

Now *I've* uncovered myself. I'm clean.

Interestingly, I've also found this process is usually safer. The shepherd-types in the congregation often keep the vultures away. If I expose my own folly, it's hard for detractors to pounce on me. Certainly this cannot become a regular ploy. But on those occasions when I have goofed and I expose myself, there's little left for my detractors to say.

It's not only a beneficial practice, it's right. When I'm at fault, I'm on far better moral footing to accept the blame rather than dodge it. People respect an honest admission of error, and even if I get some heat, I can get on with repairing the damage.

Dick Lincoln, pastor of Shandon Baptist Church in Columbia, South Carolina, interjects a word of caution, however. He believes pastors are often more sensitive to their mistakes than others are, and may be tempted to become compulsive confessors. "Many of the decisions we make are close calls. Some parts work out well, and others not so well. In many of these decisions, few people will ever think there has been a mistake without it being labeled as such. If I blunder in and tell them about the 'big mistake' I made, it may be news to them. It's a good idea to stay positive, to the extent it doesn't cloud the truth."

There's no use in sowing seeds of discontent where none would have grown on their own. A rule of thumb: Claim those obvious mistakes in the public domain. If you goofed, say so. But if a possible mistake is unclear, if it is not your fault, if it is a minor and unknown matter, then the less said, the better.

Richard Kew waited too long to claim his evident mistakes. They had mounted to such a point that the only apparent way out was to leave the ministry. However, even at this stage, the people in his church didn't pounce on him when he admitted his mistakes. Kicking a guy who just admitted he was down is not much sport.

Confessing the Failure

When the mistake is sin, pragmatic considerations are shoved aside, and confession is in order. I may need to apologize to the trustees if I show up late and unprepared for a meeting, but if I misappropriate church funds for personal use, I have two parties to appease: the board whose trust I trampled and the God whose moral law I offended.

What are the particular steps to be taken when our mistakes are of the sinful kind? When I asked one pastor, he chuckled, "Quit. You can't just sin slower!" No one can move beyond a sin that's allowed to remain habitual. Robert Millen, when finally faced with the depth of his sin, gritted his teeth and left homosexual practice cold turkey. He's celibate now, at a tremendous personal cost. When he lost everything and was alone, with only his faith and resolve to sustain him, he realized he still had to do what was right, not what was easy. He quit, and that quitting started him on the road to peace of mind.

Next, in the steps of adulterous King David who told God "You are justified when you judge" (Ps. 51:4), Robert had to confess — agree with God. He poured out his confession to God, and he bravely confessed to his family and his church, pulling no punches, shouldering full responsibility. His teenage son was crushed, and the confession neither saved his marriage nor retained his pastorate. It wasn't intended as a magical balm to salve his difficulties. It was the right and only proper course to take, difficult as it was.

For Robert, turning from the practice of sin meant a drastic alteration of his life. "I find it easier to be completely celibate," he confides, "than to be selectively celibate, so I'm not sure I could return to my wife even if she would take me back. It would open up deep reservoirs of longing I don't think I could handle."

He's fighting the battle with his homosexual orientation on a daily basis, much like an alcoholic who takes one day at a time. "I've been celibate for months," he tells me, "and I'm celibate today. I can't promise about tomorrow. I wish I could, but I can't. I know I *want* to be." He must strategize to remain pure. He has altered his lifestyle, habits, and friends in his effort to turn from sinful practice, to repent, to live his life in a way pleasing to God. He has learned the lesson: When you flee from temptation, don't leave a forwarding address.

Not all sins may be as life shattering as Robert's, but each moral mistake demands repair. Many of the pieces are in God's hands. To God we must go for confession of failure and forgiveness of sin.

The bottom line: I am accountable, and until I realize and state my accountability, I add to my mistake. But when I recognize, admit, and confess my error, I make it possible to learn and grow from it.

There are indeed wise ways to keep from making a bad situation worse, and to those we now turn.

SIX

DAMAGE CONTROL

The shortest mistakes are always the best.

MOLIÈRE

He who errs quickly, is quick in correcting the error.

FRANCIS BACON

T hick containment shields cover the best designed nuclear reactors. Should something go wrong, these shields provide the first line of defense by containing explosions, and thus contamination. If radioactive debris and gasses remain within the shield, the extent of the damage stays limited, and mop-up operations are possible.

When clergy error causes a runaway reaction in the parish, *containment* is again the word. Little mistakes have a way of becoming big, sometimes insurmountable problems — if they are not contained. Pastors have found, usually the hard way, that when the disaster alert sounds, some actions contain the damage better than others.

A Parish Chain Reaction

On a prominent suburban corner stands a beautiful church complex, newly built and lushly landscaped. Josh, the senior pastor, is a gifted preacher, a warm pastor, and a successful leader. Sitting in his finely appointed office, you get the feeling Josh must do a lot of things right.

But he made one mistake that won't let him go. Several

years back, he inadvertently stepped on the most stubborn toes ever bruised.

Those toes belonged to Tony, a man Josh helped rescue from a life of drug abuse. Once converted, Tony became a zealous church member. Initially Josh was pleased with Tony's drive, but his unbounded and erratic nature sent caution signals to Josh. Tony had plenty of free time since he was independently wealthy, and he constantly pushed Josh to be his mentor. Josh did his best to stall Tony without discouraging him. He didn't think weekly one-on-one sessions with Tony would be the best investment of his time. Tony soon realized he was being sidestepped.

Eventually Tony began to disagree with Josh over points of doctrine. Tony challenged Josh's teaching of the doctrine of the Trinity, accusing him of incipient Unitarianism. Then they clashed over spiritual gifts. Then eschatology. It degenerated into an all-out disagreement over practically everything — Josh trying to defend his theology while Tony circled and strafed whatever he considered a weak point in Josh's defense.

The confrontations started with a rather uncomfortable conversation in Josh's office. They escalated to the point that Tony rose at the close of a worship service and attacked Josh's orthodoxy before the whole congregation. Much to Tony's surprise and embarrassment, he got nowhere with the congregation. Humiliated, he kicked the dust off his sandals and tramped off to another church across town.

Over the next decade, Tony embraced and discarded at least two other congregations, but all the time he never forgot Josh. With Manson-like charisma, he gathered around him a fiercely loyal band of malcontents, and they began appearing at Josh's evening services to accost parishioners with inflammatory pamphlets Tony had produced.

Josh was upset with the way they attacked and alienated his sheep, not to mention the relentless assaults on his own leadership and integrity. He met with the group privately, to no avail. The deacons tried to arrange a conference, and were frustrated time and again. Nobody could seem to stop the incessant picking at Josh and troubling of the congregation.

The deacons drafted a letter to the congregation, explaining the disagreement, outlining their attempted resolution, and pleading for forbearance and understanding. Tony persisted in stirring trouble. Finally, the deacons arranged for a restraining order to bar Tony and his followers from church property.

That only infuriated Tony, who stepped up his tactics. He and his crew started picketing the church. Once Josh arrived at church and counted thirty-four signs denouncing him and the church posted along the sidewalk. Tony took out a half-page advertisement in the local paper. The rambling diatribe stopped only a millimeter short of slander. He peppered new church attenders with letters "warning" them about Josh.

His opposition seemed to have no limits. Once when Josh flew to Seoul, Korea, to speak at a conference, he found Tony distributing leaflets at the hall! For the last five years, Tony and his band have picketed the church every Sunday, rain or shine. He remains Josh's indefatigable albatross.

Josh lives daily with his seemingly innocuous mistake of slighting Tony that mushroomed completely out of proportion. Could it have been avoided? Josh will always wonder. But his experience illustrates the two immediate concerns that face anyone who makes a mistake: *What should I do?* and *What should I say?*

What Should I Do?

Nuclear technicians don't run to a contaminated area the minute the alarm sounds. Something dreadful has gone wrong, so now is the time for cool heads and rational problem solving. In fact, following the Three Mile Island nuclear mishap, one of the review committee's recommendations was for at least one reactor operator to be stationed away from beeping indicators and wailing sirens. Flashing lights and indicator needles in the red work against level-headed thinking. Only an untraumatized mind is able to make rapid but sound decisions. There's wisdom in this approach for pastors, too.

Proceed cautiously. Church leaders are equally wise to proceed directly yet cautiously as the warning alarms sound in the parish. A mistake triggers reaction. Things start to happen quickly, and a bigger mistake looms large when decisions are knocked off out of panic. Pastors want to avoid that.

Josh perhaps rushed to a premature decision about Tony. Tony was pushing him for the kind of mentoring Josh wasn't prepared to give. Josh's initial solution was to stall and hope Tony would give up. Instead, Tony felt offended, and trouble resulted.

When Tony started causing arguments, Josh quickly jumped in to defend himself, a natural reaction. However, as he looks back, Josh realizes that perhaps working with Tony to uncover the cause of his attacks would have been more fruitful. Josh's first response was not the best.

To help avoid making a final decision on momentary evidence, one pastor tells himself, "Nothing can be evaluated the day it happens. You can't judge the whole parade from what you see through a knothole."

Mistakes breed panic. Shutting down the decision-making process for a brief moratorium following a mistake makes good sense. This does not mean ceasing to function. It means taking time for adequate analysis.

After making a mistake, most pastors know what they *feel* — wretched. They must decide what they *know*. Josh felt upset with Tony, justifiably so. But understanding Tony was another matter. As a mistake begins to unfold, gathering information and exploring options are in order. Josh might have stopped to consider better what Tony was feeling. He could have charted his options and possible responses.

Many a resignation has been prematurely proffered, many a dream abandoned, many a blunder compounded by incautious attempts to quickly fix a mistake. A seasoned, broader perspective realizes that today's mistake may not seem so tomorrow. One pastor advises, "Give it time. I had to learn to wait on the Lord, to not make a hasty judgment. Sometimes the biggest mistake you can make is to panic and act prematurely."

Thinking through a situation adds quality to one's response. South Carolina pastor Bill Solomon cautions against overreaction: "I'm the kind of guy who goes on a ten-day fast if the doctor mentions I'm a little overweight. So when it comes to mistakes in ministry, I have to be careful not to react in inappropriate ways. Taking time to think through the situation helps. Maybe this 'disaster' is only a temporary setback, and all I need to do is hitch up my britches and keep going."

But restraint cannot mean vacillation. Eventually the time comes to act, and *eventually* usually comes sooner rather than later. A pause provides perspective; a prolonged pause leads to inaction and often breeds complications.

So when do you proceed? When you have a fair grasp of the situation and have your own emotions reasonably in check. In some cases that means counting to ten, in others, waiting ten months. Whatever the case, it means thinking first and doing second. But the time does come to act.

Proceed decisively. Josh can point to his mistake with Tony: "I didn't handle the problem properly at the beginning. I should have been more decisive. I never could have discipled Tony — that's not the point — but I should have allowed him more dignity when he first felt hurt. I could have explained my dilemma with so many people needing my attention. I could have set him up with another person in the congregation. He could have denounced me privately then and gotten it off his chest. But now he *can't* stop. He's invested too much to quit and lose face.

"I also should have recognized the meanness in human nature. Jesus dealt decisively with people, not sentimentally. When it comes to some people, I've sadly realized that if you *believe* all things, you will have all things to *endure*. I wanted to keep pleasing people — which is selfish at the core — when I should have been tougher."

After thinking through the initial course of action, steps can proceed purposefully. Encouraging them to be clear and direct, Paul wrote the Corinthians: "If the trumpet does not sound a clear call, who will get ready for battle?" (1 Cor. 14:8). Likewise, if stumbling pastors do not regain firm footing and proceed with obvious intent, who will be able to stand behind them?

One pastor of an Episcopal church allowed a difference of opinion to nearly split the congregation. Most members were staid and very conservative, and this pastor shrugged off the stir a liturgical renewal element was bringing. Even when tempers flared, accusations were hurled, and a denominational investigation was launched, the pastor remained passive, almost indifferent to the situation.

This pastor didn't react impulsively; he hardly reacted at all, and that was his greater mistake. The people needed direction, a sure trumpet. Somebody had to raise a banner. At least then people could decide whether to rally around it or consider leaving. As it was, a vacillating, inactive approach nearly doomed the church to dissolution. It wasn't until another pastor assumed command that the church began to regain some direction.

The original pastor resigned and slipped away. With clear hindsight, the present pastor told me, "I think if he would have taken a stand — practically any stand — he would still be the pastor today. The people couldn't support him because they didn't know where he stood."

Another pastor inherited a staff and ran into a problem with the man in charge of children's ministries. "He had an attitude problem," the pastor said. "Everywhere he went, he sowed dissension. We were building a new building, and he was telling the building committee one story about what he wanted in the children's center and the rest of the staff another. At the same time he was telling the teachers how he never gets anything he wants. Everybody ended up upset with everybody else because of this man.

"I kept hoping he would cooperate, but finally he sent out a letter opposing me, and our leaders and I concluded he simply could not work under my leadership. Then I made the mistake of giving him a year to find a new position. A whole year! That gave him time to continue sabotaging my ministry, like timing the announcement of his leaving to do as much damage to our building fund kickoff as possible.

"I wasn't decisive enough. By the unsure signals I kept giving out, I added to the original mistake of letting him linger. I've since decided: Make a firing quick and clean. Now I'm not saying be unfair or dictatorial. I just mean that when an original mistake in hiring becomes a major difficulty, the best move is to be decisive. Take into account their dignity, be fair, be just, but do what you have to do — let them go."

When a mistake occasions that first frantic *What do I do?* respond as the experienced do: think first and then act. Do nothing out of panic or haste, but when you do respond (and you have to eventually), act responsibly and unequivocally. As one pastor says, "You can't pussyfoot around and expect people to respect you."

What Should I Say?

There were times as a pastor when I envied the President. In his Oval Office, protected by several strata of associates and secretaries (not to mention the unsmiling guys in dark suits), he can orchestrate his response to whatever mistakes he makes. To top it off, who goes before the questioning press? Many times it's not the President. He's got a press secretary to smooth his gaffes and blunders.

For pastors, when it comes to saying the right thing following a mistake, they are on their own — no press secretaries, no high-level advisers. Along with, perhaps, a few lay leaders, they formulate their own response.

The immediate concern is *How much do I divulge? Do I go public, or should I sit on it?* In the previous chapter, we saw that the ability to own up to a mistake and call it our own is important. If it is sin, it must be confessed; if error, we need to take responsibility. Only then can we begin to fix what's "broke." But do we need to tell everybody? And how much of a mistake needs to be told?

The answers to these questions depend on at least three factors:

1. *What kind of mistake is it?* Mistakes differ by nature and magnitude. Misplacing a pencil occasions a different response than leaving the pencil imbedded in another person's chest. After the one you say, "Oops!" Following the other, you beg forgiveness.

Is it a mistake of orientation, of interpersonal relations, or of judgment? Say I come into ministry with the mistaken notion that it will be a forty-hour-a-week job, and before long I'm complaining to the board about the "unfair expectations" of the congregation. That's a mistake of orientation, and one of the best strategies is to admit my rookie notions to the board. I don't need to solemnly apologize to the whole congregation about my "grave failing." I'm learning and growing. They practically expect such mistakes, and probably take pride in "training me right." I can consider it a mistake of orientation, reorient myself, and be on my way.

But if I lash out at a distraught widow who calls me at 3 A.M. on my day off, I have injured someone and probably poisoned the interpersonal well in that congregation. I need to say more in this case — a lot more.

Within each type of mistake, magnitude determines my response. I may order church stationery with an error in the address, and in so doing, waste two hundred dollars. Or I may hire a close friend as youth director who later embezzles thousands of dollars. Both blunders were judgment mistakes, but their vastly different magnitude suggests far different responses. While I may want to mention the wasted stationery to the trustees, I may *need* to offer to step down from the pastorate in the wake of my embezzling friend.

What exactly *should* I say? It still depends. Did I know my friend was a crook and lie about it to the board when he was hired? Then I have committed not only a major mistake but a moral one, which demands asking for forgiveness. Until I understand if my error is minor, major, or moral, I don't know how much I should say.

Playground basketball games sometimes operate under the rule: No harm, no foul. If no one is hurt, no foul is called. Likewise, if no one has been truly hurt in a church situation, pastors need not blow the whistle on themselves.

Some mistakes hardly merit disclosure. Must I bring to the board every undiplomatic word I let slip, every phone call I forget to return, every errant thought about that attractive gal in the supermarket? Must I confess from the pulpit those two hours I wasted in my study reading *Life* magazine, or the time I snarled at the C.E. director who forgot to give me the attendance figures for the third week in a row? Of course not. Common sense tells us to measure the exposure of the mistake by its nature and magnitude. Big sins demand more said than minor slips.

In a way this runs contrary to our inclinations. It's the major failings I'd just as soon bandage over and forget. But it's exactly those mistakes that hurt the most that have to be exposed for healing. The little scratches will take care of themselves, but the deep wounds need open attention.

All the same, one pastor says, "I try to admit my mistakes in a way that is not heavy on guilt. If I've done wrong, I say so, but I don't try to make myself look like a no-good rat. I'll talk to the person my mistake affects and apologize for the action — sincerely. But I don't need to apologize for what or who I am. That can overwhelm even the one I'm talking to."

2. *Who is involved?* Recognizing three possibilities helps us sort out this question.

Sometimes I'm the only one fumbling the ball. Maybe I don't study enough for my sermons or I'm always late for work. Perhaps I short my prayer life. These are personal in nature; I'm acting in collusion with no one.

Whatever I say about this kind of mistake, I am the only person exposed. In considering the wisdom of confessing my sin or admitting my error, I have no co-conspirators to think about. Some of these mistakes can be corrected with a little resolve, and I need to decide the advisability of involving others at all.

Why expose my lack of devotional time to the congregation? Wouldn't it be better to tell one or two persons whom I could ask to hold me accountable? Then, while I work to mend the error under their supervision, I haven't undermined my position or unnecessarily burdened people with my shortcoming that they may well use as an excuse for theirs — "After all, if the pastor has trouble . . ."

Those errors in which only I am involved are sometimes best left in a small, chosen circle.

Other mistakes pit me against personalities: stubbornly contradicting a founding member or demanding Gaither anthems from a popular choir director whose tastes run toward Bach. Such interpersonal mistakes become more complex, because now I'm dealing with the rights and emotions of others. I need to judge what to say not only by how it affects me but by how others are affected by it.

Will I make others look bad if I go public? Will it cause them to feel they have to reciprocate? Would the problem best be settled in private with the other party?

Most of us have heard the "confession" that is really a thinly veiled attack: "I'm so sorry I punched Deacon Tidwell at the last deacons' meeting. After he had been so tightfisted when discussing my salary, and when he viciously tried to take away my car allowance, I guess I just cracked." It is tempting to wallop someone again under the guise of admitting a mistake.

Still other mistakes involve co-conspirators. When somebody else has joined me in the mistake, that party is bound to be implicated by any statement I make. I may be ready to go public, but is he or she?

When Josh and Tony scrapped over doctrine, Josh was probably making a mistake by allowing it to degenerate into personal attacks. But so was Tony. Thus anything Josh had to say about the problem to the deacons or congregation involved Tony as much as himself. Josh could own up to the mistake or confess the sin *for himself*, but not at Tony's expense. Whatever Josh said about Tony had to be fair and truthful, not just another way to spar with him. In situations like this, restraint and diplomacy are the key words; not cover-up, but tact.

3. *Who needs to know?* The key word here is *needs*. All kinds of people may want to hear about a mistake, but not everybody has a stake in my revelation. Running out on the street and pouring out my shortcomings to the first passerby hardly suffices as a confession. Yet, in some cases, mounting the pulpit to spew a confession to the congregation may be just as inappropriate. In general, mistakes should be broadcast no farther than the narrowest necessary circle.

So who belongs in that circle? Any person involved in my mistake. I need to come clean with those affected. Greg Ogden needed to talk with his senior pastor to clear the breach he'd caused by his smugness. Robert Millen faced a wrenching session with his wife and family when his homosexuality was discovered. They were victims of the mistake; they deserved a full explanation, if not more.

In nearly any instance when the organization suffers from my mistake, key church leaders need to be brought into the circle of confidence. After all, they share responsibility for the welfare of the congregation. In a support staff position, this would include the senior pastor. In other churches, the moderator, the chairman of the board, the executive committee of the elders, or other such individuals might be the first people to contact. They can help decide how much wider the spotlight of revelation has to shine.

If the key leaders are able to receive the disclosure of misconduct and deal with it effectively, perhaps that's as wide an exposure as is necessary. The purpose is health and repair. Hidden sin is usually growing sin. Unacknowledged error is often repeated error. Airing the mistake before those who need to know, taking steps to rectify the wrong and forestall repetition, and then getting on with business — that's the order of the day. If a small but responsible group can accomplish that purpose, most pastors are ahead to let it remain there.

Sometimes, however, due to the nature or magnitude of a mistake, the exposure needs to be greater — the entire leadership of the congregation, or perhaps the entire congregation. In Colorado an assistant pastor was caught embezzling checks from the offering. Eventually not only the leadership but the congregation and finally the community played a role in rectifying this mistake. His church board was forced by state law to report his theft of corporate funds to the state's attorney. Even though they wanted word of the regrettable occurrence to go no further, it became public record by necessity. The remorseful assistant is now back in the congregation after serving a jail sentence for grand theft.

Josh used this narrowest-circle method. First he tried to pacify Tony. When that didn't work, he talked with key church leaders. They decided the deacons as a whole needed to be briefed. Only when even the deacons couldn't contain the difficulty did Josh and the leaders attempt to communicate the problem to the entire congregation.

As chaplain for a small-town police force, I was occasionally subpoenaed to testify in court concerning incidents I had witnessed while riding with officers. On the way to my first courtroom appearance, a friend in the department offered some sound advice: "Never volunteer information. Answer the questions, but don't say anything you don't have to say. It can keep you out of a lot of trouble." He wasn't telling me to lie or to duck questions; he only advised restraint. Why buy trouble with unnecessary jabber?

Pastors can learn from that officer's advice. Following a mistake, *something* needs to be said — even volunteered — something truthful and upright. Conscience, good faith, and Christian maturity demand it. But the amount said and the audience told are best limited by the scope of the mistake: Say no more than is necessary to no greater audience than the mistake merits.

SEVEN

A MISTAKE OR NOT?

If it was an error, its causes were honorable.

OVID

T

hose who commit first-class blunders and blatant sins usually know it, and can begin to work on them. But sometimes the categories blur and the markings of a genuine mistake become indistinct. Is everything that appears to be a mistake a mistake?

Alan Taylor felt he was growing fat at First Presbyterian Church in Auburn, California. Not that he was putting on weight; Alan's trim, well-groomed appearance spoke quietly of accomplishment. He suspected his ministry was assuming the indolent ease.

His nine years in Auburn, a burgeoning Sierra foothill community where forty-niners once panned for gold, had been happy. Maybe too happy. After unbroken success, Alan began to wonder, *Am I becoming content to relax and enjoy the journey?* His people freely expressed their affection for the Taylors, giving them tickets to the Sacramento Symphony and the use of ski condos at Lake Tahoe. Alan could never be called a freeloader. First Church had grown from four hundred to nearly a thousand under his leadership. But his tendency to reside in the ease of a comfortable position disturbed him.

Writing had provided Alan's recent excitement. His two books produced speaking engagements and ego strokes. Writing stimulated him, while the church remained a predictable, mastered enterprise.

"I don't want to just be coasting in my forties," he confided to his wife, Sue. "I need to stay alive, to be challenged by my ministry, not just by my next book."

Alan's daughter contributed to his growing restlessness. "For fifteen years Nikki was a kid you'd want to order from a catalogue," Alan explains. "She was everything you could want." But adolescence didn't treat her gently. Boys twice broke her heart, she was cut from a team, and, in her failing self-esteem, she took up with the wrong crowd at school. In a year's time, Nikki degenerated from the perfect child to the epitome of a troubled teen.

The Taylors agonized over every turn for the worse. After an all-night escapade with a boy they had forbidden Nikki to see, the fallout included her extreme rebellion and sullenness. Alan and Sue became frantic. Something had to be done for Nikki — and for the *family!* "If we can only get her out of town," Alan suggested to Sue, "if we can extract her from the chain of negative elements, Nikki might have a chance."

Enter Broadmoor Presbyterian Church of Seattle. Ralph Bates, the chairman of the pastor nominating committee, had appreciated Alan's books. He called Alan, and as they talked over the phone, he said he considered Alan a dynamic "name" pastor able to lend prestige to Broadmoor Presbyterian.

The church was a proud dowager, existing on a handsome endowment and waning reputation. Ralph could remember when it was *the* church in Seattle. At one time the university president, the mayor, and half the physicians at Harborview Hospital were members. However, the last seventeen years witnessed an exodus of members as Dr. Hedgepath had occupied the pulpit with friendly gentility but ebbing effectiveness.

Ralph figured the church needed a shot in the arm, and Alan Taylor was the man to do it. He and two others flew to Sacramento to talk with Alan. Alan met them at the airport and took them to Old Sacramento for lunch.

Ralph painted a glowing picture of Broadmoor Presbyterian: its grand history, the beautiful Gothic sanctuary, and its pivotal role in meeting Seattle's needs. Then he turned to Alan and flatly declared, "I believe you're just the man we need to restore the eminence of our church." The other two committee members looked surprised by Ralph's license, but Alan was hooked by the challenge.

They spent the better part of a day talking about the church and Alan's strengths in ministry. The delegation returned to Seattle convinced they had their man, and that evening Alan rejoiced with Sue over the exciting prospects. After the Taylors' candidating trip to Seattle that took on the air of a royal visit, the pieces all fell into place. Alan announced his resignation in Auburn, and the Taylors were warmly feted and graciously released. By summer they were ensconced in a Seattle home with a view of Mount Rainier.

Excitement bubbled in the Taylor household — until the first Session meeting. Alan was completely unprepared for what transpired: "I expected some kind of jockeying for position over who runs the church. Usually the elders take an initial wait-and-see approach, but not at Broadmoor. Ralph Bates tied into me that very first meeting."

Dr. Jekyll came on like Mr. Hyde. "Alan," Ralph chided, "who gave you permission to change our worship? You may have played fast and loose in laid-back California, but this is *Broadmoor*. Traditions mean something here."

Is this the same guy who told me Broadmoor needed changes? Alan wondered. *What gives? All I did was move the announcements to the beginning of the service.* Alan backpedaled. "Ralph, I'm confused. I didn't mean to step on any toes, but I thought from our conversations in Sacramento that Broadmoor was ripe for innovation." *And why a public forum to upbraid me?*

Ralph responded with an air of innocence. "I'm sorry if you were misled, but we need some stability now, not a lot of new ideas floating around."

Who did he think misled me? Alan wondered. He felt the victim of false advertising.

The reality of Broadmoor Presbyterian, at least as Ralph

Bates now painted it, was not at all to Alan's liking. He had come to give strong, innovative leadership to a church wandering in a muddle. That enticed him. But this?

On the way out of the meeting, Ralph steered Alan into a corner. "Alan," he whispered, "what you want to do, this church needs. But wait. Let me be a buffer for you; lay low for a while."

"But that's not me. I've always been a strong leader, and this place *needs* a leader. In two years, it could go totally dormant!"

"Alan, I know this church. Don't upset the gentry. We'll all look bad."

"I'll think about it" was all Alan could promise. *So now he wants me to chaplain the status quo, does he? And why was the rest of the Session so strangely silent?*

Alan had enjoyed warm relationships with the chairmen of previous calling committees. They had become his best friends who stood with him in difficult times. In Seattle, Ralph Bates proved his chief antagonist, opposing Alan at every turn. It disheartened Alan as their views of the church and Alan's role in it clashed like two air masses over Kansas.

Other unexpected problems fell on Alan with the leaves of fall. The church ethos differed from Auburn to Seattle. In California the people represented a plethora of backgrounds, so no one way of doing things prevailed. Not so in Seattle. The congregation of Broadmoor Presbyterian cherished long-established expectations. This caught Alan off guard.

For instance, an unwritten assumption governed staff size: There shall never be more ministers than when old Dr. Kennedy was pastor in the glory days of the late fifties. If he could handle things with two associates, so can anyone else.

For Alan, adding staff back at First Church had been a management matter, not a visceral statement. He couldn't live with such an arbitrary imposition. He informed the Session, "I need another staff pastor. Three of us cannot adequately meet the needs of a two-thousand-member congregation, especially if we intend to grow!" Ralph opposed it vigorously, but the Session eventually approved it. The feeling was, "You're the new pastor; we'll go with you this time and see what happens." Although he won the battle, Alan had shed some blood on the battlefield, and he had never been wounded like that before.

What have I done here? he wondered. *Did I panic and bolt when I should have stayed put in Auburn? Did I make a decision in the midst of emotional turmoil and turn off my brain in the process? Was I making God's decisions for him? And if so, is all this the result of my disobedience?*

A second front drained Alan's resources from the church battles: Nikki did not take the move well. Seattle was not her home. She missed the hot summers and the inner tube runs down the American River. Too insecure to make new friends in an established social climate, Nikki retreated into her bitterness over what had been "done to her."

Throughout the summer Nikki coped by sleeping fourteen hours a day. With school in September, her passive symptoms of depression turned active. "Mom," she ventured one day dragging in from a terrible day at school, "you and Dad would be a lot better off without me, wouldn't you?"

Sue was startled. "What do you mean by that?"

"It's just that I'm such a loser. If I were dead, you wouldn't have to bother with me any more."

"Nikki, that's not at all true, and you know it!" Sue was stunned, but when she found a large bottle of sleeping pills squirrelled away in Nikki's dresser, she and Alan hurried her to a psychiatrist. Afraid they might lose Nikki, they wondered, *Have we made a fatal error?*

The combination of Nikki's troubles and the dashing of expectations for the church shook Alan. The excitement of the move had bleached out in the first wash. With Ralph nipping at his heels like a hyperactive sheep dog, the Session meetings drained Alan. The people seemed cold and distant, as if they were waiting to pass judgment on what this bigshot from California could perform.

"By December," Alan recalls, "I was one day away from

leaving the ministry. I contacted a friend in business to see if I might do something besides preaching. If somebody had come along with an offer, I'd have been gone." The gray Seattle days obscured his view of Mount Rainier.

Alan's problem with Ralph, although unexpected, was probably inevitable. Fortunately Ralph exercised considerably more sway in the church Alan came to than in the one Alan eventually fashioned. Ralph's star gradually faded as Alan's ascended. But Alan couldn't initially foresee that.

In the midst of his distress, Alan took some missteps. "I became impatient," he recalls. "I forced almost immediate changes. I later counted thirty-one changes in the first year alone — big things like raising the budget and proposing new staff. Somehow we survived, but the changes came more because of my ego needs than church needs. Since I had made a mistake in coming, I felt I had to make the shoe fit *me* — and fast — just to survive."

One fellow stomped into Alan's office and said, "You've stolen our church!"

"Whose church?"

"Our church," he replied.

"Yours?" asked Alan. "Who owns it?"

"Those of us who started it," he grumped.

Alan's counter, "We're Christ's church," rang a little empty with all his maneuvering.

Such was the resistance he encountered with the charter members. Only Alan's pulpit effectiveness and his credentials from many years of pastoral experience covered for his over-zealousness to "shape up the church."

Alan began recovering from his mistake in pain's forced self-examination. *What am I in this thing for? Is it pleasure? Recognition? Maybe I was spoiled in Auburn. Titus was surrounded by liars and gluttons; maybe this is my Island of Crete. Who am I to say there's not some reason for my going through this?*

He also took refuge in his marriage. Sue shared the trauma over Nikki and much of the shock of going from a loving, affirming congregation to a more standoffish group. Together they endured what they called "a major change in temperature from a warm shower to a cold."

Eventually the cold shower warmed. Alan's humor and warmth lodged in the congregation and started reflecting back on him and his family. People reached out individually. "We started getting dinner invitations," Alan remembers. "Then we heard that nearly one hundred had gathered in a home to pray for us and communicate support when rumor had it we were unsettled."

People broke through the cold barriers Alan originally felt. "They gave encouragement enough that I could take the next step until finally I could start walking again" is how Alan put it. That second wind kept him from gasping for oxygen elsewhere.

One of Alan's heroes, a retired saint, buoyed him. "Alan," he said, "there isn't one church reaching Seattle like you can." To Alan that was like saying "Sic 'em" to a dog. It gave him a challenge; it helped him look outside himself. Perhaps pride had something to do with it, but it rekindled Alan's vision.

Later, visitors from his Auburn parish told him, "Now we see why God led you here. Though we miss you, we realize this is a place where you can really minister." They perceived what Alan, in his struggle, was missing: his "mistake" was not without redeeming factors. Their encouragement added a page of affirmation to a narrow volume.

Probably the pew-to-pulpit communication accomplished the greatest remedial work. "Every preacher receives communication from the pew while he preaches, both good and bad," Alan observes. "The pew was my sustaining grace. I was saved by the timely comfort telegraphed by people inspired by God." In doing the work of the ministry, Alan began to receive the rewards, even when interspersed with brickbats from other quarters.

No dramatic turns catapulted the Taylors into bliss. For many months they lived day to day with the dreary results of a decision that for all the world sure *felt* like a mistake. With an occasional tactical victory in Session, with a rising incidence of pleasant encounters with parishioners, with a rare period of sunshine in Nikki's struggle, with the belief that God intends to mend mistakes, but mostly with dogged determination not to stumble recklessly into another blunder, Alan, Sue, and even Nikki weathered that Seattle move.

Three years later, with the church once again a sound vessel on a new course, Alan breathes a sigh of relief, cautiously thankful he didn't jump ship in the rough waters.

Was It a Mistake?

Did Alan make a mistake going to Broadmoor? Three months after arriving in Seattle, Alan wanted to abandon the ministry altogether. "I thought getting Nikki out of Auburn would be good for her," Alan explains. "I thought a new challenge would stimulate me. I was wrong. I had used the wrong criteria to force a move. Maybe I was trying to make God's plan fit my expectations.

"Yet, I believe if I am sincere despite the emotional trauma I am under, if I am following the light as best I know how, even if I make a mistake, God will rescue me. And I'll grow through it."

That's exactly what happened to Alan in Seattle. "The church will never become completely what I expected, and I doubt Ralph will ever be on my side. But he's coming around. After playing left field without a mitt for three years, maybe he's beginning to understand the rest of the team is following the coach's direction."

For agonizing months it had all the symptoms of a colossal mistake. But is something a mistake that begins like a mistake, develops like a mistake, and feels like a mistake, even when it doesn't end a horrendous mistake? Perhaps God's very ability to redeem our blunders colors the picture in hindsight.

"Who knows when to measure a mistake?" Alan muses. "Do you measure it when you first go to town and they stone you, like they did Paul? Or do you stick around and build a church? Broadmoor is a different church now than it was a few years back, but it takes a lot longer to turn a big ship than it does a rowboat."

Alan *is* happy now — challenged, successful, and satisfied — without having abandoned Broadmoor Presbyterian. He wouldn't choose to go through the wringer again, nor would he recommend subjecting a troubled teen to Nikki's ordeal. Yet the God who reconciled Paul and Barnabas, who redeemed the libertine Augustine, who recommissioned the failed missionary John Wesley, who recovered conspirator Charles Colson — *that* God habitually uses even our seeming mistakes for his purposes.

Alan stayed at Broadmoor. Others leave their churches when the signs point toward an error. How do you know which course is best?

EIGHT

TO FIGHT OR TO FLEE?

When people once are in the wrong,
Each line they add is much too long;
Who fastest walks, but walks astray,
Is only furthest from his way.

MATTHEW PRIOR

Half the failures in life arise from pulling
in one's horse as he is leaping.

J. C. and A. W. HARE

Our cat made a mistake. The neighbor's kitchen door was open, and it must have appeared inviting, because Katie Cat went in to explore. When our neighbor, Mike, found her on the kitchen counter, Katie sensed her guilt. In a flash she flew upstairs and found the first available hiding place: under the bed.

Mike's a nice guy. He just planned to reach under the bed, pick up Katie, and take her outside where she belonged. No malice; no problem. Katie wasn't so charitable.

In a dark corner, backed against a wall, Katie, the gentle kitty who purrs on laps, reverted to feral ferociousness. She clamped her teeth onto Mike's thumb and raked his hands with her claws. As Mike pulled free, she took off — climbing the drapes, leaping against the window, and tearing around the room with unbelievable energy. Caught in a mistake, sure her world had narrowed to this harrowing moment, Katie turned into a terror.

To fight or to flee — most of us face the decision at one time or another. Following a mistake, especially a big mistake, the choice almost always demands a decision.

Once you've faced up to a mistake, straightened things out

with God, contained the damage, and said what needed to be said, you're stuck with a decision: *Do I — can I — stay in this church, or must I leave?* Often it's a tough call. Both solutions commend themselves, and with good reason.

If a pastor has any sense of accomplishment in a congregation, leaving following a mistake paints a once-colorful picture black. "The Flight of the Bumbling Me" is not the kind of exit music most pastors want. None of us likes to depart a loser. We'd rather stay and eventually exit a winner.

Yet to remain where you're considered a buffoon or a crook or a pervert — with or without justification — is sheer agony. You have a reputation to undo, people to appease, confidence to rebuild. Perhaps in that setting you'll always be "the guy who bankrupted First Church." So what do you do?

Here's what some pastors who have been through the process have to say.

Reasons to Leave

There are several possible reasons to leave.

You're unwanted. One pastor, whose immorality ushered him out of one congregation and whose second pastorate ended abruptly following a leak about the first, advised, "There's a definite sign that says to leave: when the people don't want you anymore. That's the determining factor, not the type of mistake or the magnitude of it. After all, what's more serious, gossip or adultery? The magnitude is a cultural distinction. They're both sin. And if you've already built a loving relationship with the congregation, you can weather almost any mistake. Then people want you to stay, if only for your own healing.

"But you're a fool to stay where you're not wanted. Even Jesus said to brush the dust off your feet."

But what about split decisions — some beg you to stay and others insist that you leave? It depends on the severity of the split.

The pastor gives two examples: "I was discovered in an

adulterous relationship in the first church, and the church council voted unanimously to fire me. I had no choice; I went to the business meeting and handed in my resignation. They told me to leave town, not to set foot in the church again. There was nothing split about that decision.

"Then fifteen months after we went to another church, that congregation asked me to leave, basically because I had not informed the entire congregation of the whole story of why I had left the first church. I had never trusted them with that information because I was sure they would ask me to resign!

"But this time the board stood behind me. I had told them all the facts from the beginning, and they were 100 percent with me. They were ready to go to bat for me. But I resigned anyway. I could see that to stay would have meant splitting the church, and I didn't want to do that. You can't force your ministry on people. If they don't want you, then go; your ministry there is over."

You're not trusted. Sometimes the people still like you after you've let them down. This is more likely after a poor decision than after a moral failure. You've blown it, but nobody's vindictive. They're not ready to wash their hands of you. You've been their pastor, and the warm bond still means something.

But they've lost confidence in you. They may love you, but they don't trust you.

Pastors work overtime to build people's confidence in their personal integrity, their understanding of godly (and appropriate earthly) things. After all, who will respect the knowledge of a pastor who thinks Sartre was an "exosensualist"? Or who will take the premarital counsel of the minister whose family is in shambles? The perceived level of maturity and competence on a number of measures can make or break a pastor's ministry.

When a pastor errs, some people never forget it. If it is a major error, confidence in the pastor can be washed out, and ministry gets mired to the axles amid dubious parishioners.

A Southern Baptist pastor put it this way: "You can pass a

point of no return, and the trust factor is gone. Then you can no longer command the kind of respect you need. You become muted, and once you're muted, you have no ministry. Your only alternative is to leave.

"There's a difference in congregations, though. You take a highly legalistic congregation that lives by the letter of the law: sneeze at the Communion table and you've lost their confidence. They'll hang you after your first mistake.

"But some congregations have reputations for being loving. They want to believe in a person; they'll build you up. We have a youth minister whose wife left him. It broke his heart, and I thought, *It'll be interesting to see what happens here.* Our youth committee gave him 100 percent support. He got nothing but strokes of love. 'Don't leave us,' they said. 'We're going to help you through this thing whether she comes back or not.' She's back now, and they're reconciled. But the church never lost confidence in this young man. It would have compounded the tragedy had he been forced out."

Jerry Hayner, pastor of Forest Hills Baptist Church in Raleigh, North Carolina, compares the pastor to a football coach: "You can't let the people lose confidence in your leadership. Once they think you're not a competent signal-caller, or you're not showing the necessary good judgment to win the ball game, the magic is no longer there. Once you cross that line, you have to be nothing less than Jesus Christ to come back across it. The people have written you off."

You run out of fight. A pastor accepted a call to a church with 99 percent of the congregation affirming his call. In spite of the church's history of "losing" its pastors after about three years, he assumed whatever problems had existed would not necessarily resurface. That was not the case. A handful of strong-willed elders lay in wait to challenge his authority.

Within a year they were harping about "not being fed" by his preaching. He met with them and tried everything he knew to meet their expectations. After three years of struggle, he thought the relationship was finally improving, and he began to breathe a little easier. In a matter of weeks, he was stunned by a call for his resignation.

He probably could have marshaled the troops for a battle. His mistakes had been minor: some ill-considered words, not confronting the troublemakers directly enough, perhaps coming to the church in the first place. Yes, the church had lost a few people, but that's not unusual with a new pastor, and the situation had stabilized. The congregation had even gained new members who were excited about the church. The majority of the congregation had no idea what was going on in the elders meetings.

Although the pastor had done nothing worthy of being fired, he quietly resigned. Sometimes you have no more fight left. He walked out of the last elders meeting with the parting words: "When you leave, please unplug the coffee pot."

His decision was uncomplicated: "I'm sure, if I had felt strongly enough about it, I could have fought and perhaps won. But after three years of struggle, what would I have gained? If they all resigned and left the church, it would have been difficult to go on. But if they had remained at the church, I didn't see how I could keep going on. I no longer wanted to fight."

A significant — even a beatable — opposition often places a pastor in a no-win situation. Even if you win the battle to stay, you end up pastoring a crippled church. There are times to concede it's not worth the damage. As one pastor noted, "Once I resigned, the church was free to fight over principles and not personalities. I think the right side is going to win, but my presence would have muddied the waters."

A cartoon depicts a soot-covered man in rags peering out on a countryside ravaged by atomic war. The caption reads, "We won — I think." For their own sake and for the welfare of their churches, many pastors will leave a church, choosing not to submit everyone to a battle resulting at best in a nebulous victory.

You need a fresh start. The pastor mentioned in chapter three who became overly involved in his wife's soap-selling venture got to the point where he was embarrassed by his reputation.

He was delighted to accept a call to a new community where he could be free of any taint. He might have quit hawking soap in his original parish, but he never could have washed his hands of his image in that community. It took a new church in a distant place to give him a clean start.

Pastors' mistakes of orientation may follow them throughout their tenure in a community. A pastor perceived as uncaring at her first funeral in a new church may wear the insensitive label as long as she stays in that parish. The one who pushed too hard at the beginning may always be considered aggressive. Sometimes pastors get off on the wrong foot with a key personality in the church, and everything is rocky from then on, no matter how hard they try to rectify their mistakes.

In situations like these, throwing in the towel is wisdom, not defeat. Nothing is particularly noble about remaining in an unproductive situation, especially one of your own making, when your gifts and energy can be productive elsewhere. "You don't know how good it feels finally to be appreciated," one pastor told me, "especially after the beating I took the last four years. I don't know why I took so long to make the change."

Your repentance needs to be demonstrated. When the failure is moral offense, often a trial period apart from church responsibilities is a wise course of action. This allows the fallen leader to reestablish moral roots and public credibility.

A young pastor fell into an adulterous relationship with a woman in his congregation. When it was discovered, his wife left him and he resigned his church. He's under the wing of a caring congregation now, and they have every intention of reaffirming his call to ministry and even helping establish him in a new congregation. Yet, during this year-long hiatus, he's working as a construction laborer. This work with his hands is not so much penance as therapy. It allows him to make a new start after his mistake, to order and discipline his life that ministry might resume.

"Discretion is the better part of valor," or so goes the saying. Some battle lines should never be drawn, some battles never fought. Sometimes emptying your files and leaving graciously is the best course of action following a mistake. But not always.

Reasons to Remain

Mistakes don't always signal the end of a ministry. If every pastor who made a mistake were finished, we should all buy stock in Allied Van Lines. Staff directories would be on chalkboards, because everyone would be moving.

Thankfully, not every mistake is fatal. The reasons for staying — even after a major mistake — often overwhelm those for leaving. Every day, pastors are retaining their positions in order to live through and grow beyond their mistakes. So what signals the time to remain rather than relocate?

The people want you to stay. This first reason may appear obvious, but to those in the throes of error, it is not always so. Within one's heart, it's easy to say, *I'm finished. Nobody will take me after this.*

At the same time, a loving congregation might be thinking, *We're sorry Bob's blown it, but he's still our pastor. We can forgive him. Let's get beyond this mistake and back to ministry.*

A congregation rallying behind their pastor is so different from the one preparing to ride him out of town. Yet at just the moment when a pastor's conscience or pride is wounded, reading the intentions of the congregation is often difficult. A sense of failure may distort perceptions of the minds and actions of parishioners. The group ready to forgive is imagined to be ready to mutiny. Jumping ship appears the only course of action, when a willing crew would rather ride out the storm with their captain.

"Never underestimate the power of a congregation to forgive," advises one pastor. "Yes, congregations can be stiff opponents, but so many really want to support their pastors, even when they obviously err. I think a pastor can live down just about any mistake — *if* the congregation is with him."

The immediate and "honorable" pastoral resignation will sometimes be refused. "Tom, we love you too much to let you go," said one congregation when their pastor tendered his resignation following a botched building program. "We won't accept your resignation. We want you to stay here, and we'll lick this thing together."

Resignation is a final step. Prior to that resignation, hopefully the pastor has taken time to discern the signs of congregational support. Some questions to consider:

— Am I able to separate my feelings about myself from what I perceive the congregation feels? Am I hearing what they are saying or what I expect them to say?

— How many of the notes, calls, and comments are sympathetic? How many are hostile?

— Has anybody asked me to stay? Are there any indications of congregational warmth and support?

— What do the opinion setters — the "tribal chiefs" in the congregation — think about my staying? Do I have them on my side?

— Does this congregation have a history of nursing the wounded or shooting them?

— Do people view my staying as helping or hindering the mission of this congregation?

One pastor said, "My most important ministry has been making up for my early mistakes in the pastorate and not moving elsewhere." Ministry can continue, perhaps even flourish, under the care of a wounded healer.

Jerry Hayner remarks, "The ministers I've seen who were willing to be human beings with feet of clay, who shared their pain and their mistakes to help their congregations avoid those same problems, have stayed on. Their churches have not accepted their resignations, and they've continued on to have successful pastorates."

This much is certain: one cannot remain effective without the support of the leadership and congregation. With it, however, staying is often the best choice.

You want to weather the storm and later leave confidently. Quick flight may actually work damage. It confirms people's worst suspicions and the pastor's sense of failure. If the ship appears sound, staying to ride out the gale can be a positive move, even if the eventual intention is to seek another call when the seas die down.

A pastor tells of a man who stayed to live down his mistake: "When I was in college, rumors began fluttering around that this pretty little woman in the church had the pastor in her bedroom. I found it hard to believe — not *this* man! And that's the way a lot of people felt, but there was evidence that seemed to indicate at least the strong possibility that it happened.

"It was never really proven, but the rumor was so strong the truth mattered little. People were going to believe what they wanted to believe. A lot of preachers would have shoved off, but he didn't. He maintained his innocence with the deacons, with small groups, and with individuals. He never took it into the pulpit. He never said, 'There are liars in this community!' or that sort of thing. Instead, he just preached the best he'd ever preached. The church actually prospered. He stayed and won his battle. There are times when you can.

"Later he resigned with dignity and went on to a big-city pastorate for several years. He finished up his ministry not far from the first church. He's retired now, revered in his own church and beloved in the whole area. He outlived the stigma. He didn't leave the area until he did."

Why did it work for this pastor when others have been sent packing? He had a mostly loving church he had pastored effectively for a number of years. And things went well, even as the rumors circulated. Had the church taken a nose-dive, the pastor would likely not have survived.

Was he guilty? "He never admitted it," recalls his friend. "In fact, he told me one time that he didn't do it. He said, 'I was indiscreet, yes; but sexually involved, no.' But I don't know." It's a complicated case. *Should* he have stayed? The jury is out. He did stay, however, and both the church and his ministry appear stronger for the decision.

Remaining brings the possibility of better results. Leaving can often appear easier. You're gone. You can put the mistake behind you and start over. Maybe word of it won't follow into your new situation. Cutting and running looks good when the debris of a mistake comes crashing down. But the immediate temptation to flee needs to be resisted. Leaving can set back the ministry of a church and place your future in jeopardy.

One veteran pastor says, "Just because we have pain in the Christian life doesn't mean we are outside the will of God. You look through Christian history — Jesus, Paul, Peter, Martin Luther, and the rest — and if people had decided there can't be pain in the will of God, where would we be?"

A pastor friend of mine went to a small church that had been withering under a leader coasting toward retirement. This new pastor brought creative ideas and energy into this, his second charge. He had plans for effective evangelism, revitalizing the Sunday school, and building a new building. For a while, it looked like he just might make it happen. Then, after eighteen months, I got a phone call from him.

"I'm resigning," he said, and the flatness of his voice told me the rest. A small group of the old-timers, people actually on the fringe of the newly vital church, had engineered a midnight massacre. They started rumors of discontent, blew the situation out of proportion, and cast such fear of a church battle into their pastor's mind that he capitulated without a defense. He handed in a letter of resignation and slipped out of the role of pastor onto the rolls of general assistance. I sometimes saw him as he picked up groceries for his family from the community food pantry, and a couple of years later, this injured man was gardening and teaching sporadically to make ends meet.

It was a classic example of a church where the wrong side prevailed. After my friend left, the church struggled merely to remain viable; yet before the blowup and resignation, it looked like they would go somewhere. Now their life together is covered with a cloud of despair. They don't feel good about what they did to their pastor, and the community remembers them as "the church that sacked their preacher." Nobody won. Even the disgruntled faction faded back into disinterest.

I often wonder what would have happened had my friend fought the opposition. Surely he was not perfect. He had made his share of mistakes. But the magnitude of the mistakes hardly warranted his firing. As it turned out, a majority of the church liked his leadership. As messy as a church battle might have become, as painful as it might have been for my friend and his family, I expect he would have emerged the victor, and, more importantly, the church might have continued to reach out. His hasty exit — overnight, in fact — impoverished his family, crippled the church, and allowed the wrong side to claim victory.

Sometimes after an initial setback, you size up your forces and stay for the battle. Principle overrides the avoidance of pain.

Personal Factors

Whether a pastor ultimately resigns or stays, personal and family needs must be factored into the decision.

Some personality types are better equipped for heroic stands. Such pastors thrive on challenge; in difficulty, they produce beyond themselves. Other pastors wither under criticism and conflict; they flourish in a tranquil situation others consider dull. One's strengths and capabilities help determine the decision to fight or to flee.

In a survey reported by Terry Muck in *When to Take a Risk*, more pastors who stayed after a tough decision reported that it taxed their health than pastors who were actually fired. In their estimation, those who stayed endured more personal pain.

Gordon Weekley resigned his church in Charlotte when he finally realized the extent of his drug addiction. He had a chemical enemy to fight, and that gave him nothing left to pastor a church — at least for a while. As much as the church loved him, they accepted that resignation. Gordon was bankrupt, his pastoral resources spent. For his sake, and for the welfare of the church, he needed to resign.

Perhaps my friend mentioned above who capitulated to the minority knew himself better than anyone else. Perhaps he knew that no matter what the odds, he could not have survived the fracas. If so, his resignation was wise. Broken, he would have been of little use to anyone.

On the other hand, Alan Taylor stuck out a rough period at Broadmoor Presbyterian. At one point he was convinced he had blundered badly by removing himself from a comfortable pastorate and immersing himself in a misunderstanding. But he wisely realized some things work out over time. He has spent several years now at Broadmoor, and he grows more satisfied with the position daily. He didn't leave; he paid the price — one he figured he could bear — and he survived.

The cost to family is also a consideration for pastors. No pastor wants to put his family through unnecessary unpleasantness. In Terry Muck's survey, pastors who had been fired considered the cost to their children slightly higher than if they had stayed and taken the heat, although both options occasioned considerable unhappiness. Since the same fired pastors counted their personal pain less than had they stayed, it appears the easier route for the pastor may actually be the more painful for the family.

Stories of pastors' children sitting through congregational meetings as their fathers are skewered make any parent shudder. Pastors want to avoid such ugly confrontations for their families. Yet, it's no church picnic for a child to be uprooted under unhappy circumstances, leave friends, and deal with a parent's defeat. Both leaving and staying can expose spouse and children to unpleasant circumstances.

To help make an informed decision about the effects of fighting or fleeing, pastors sort through questions like these:

— If I stay and work through my mistake, is this the kind of congregation that can get ugly? Are my spouse and children apt to be subjected to vicious parishioners? Or is this a forgiving, caring congregation intent on helping us all through a difficult time?

— How will my decision affect the security of my family? Do we have a place to go? Will I be able to find suitable employment?

— If we stay, will the community be as accepting as the congregation? In town, what will my wife be forced to bear? Or my children at school?

— If we go, will my family take with them a sense of defeat? How will our decision affect our children's sense of self-worth, their attitude toward the church and the faith, and their esteem of their pastor/parent?

— How much of the decision should we share with our children? What are they old enough to understand and bear? When *do* we share the whole story with them?

— Do we have family consensus on what is *right?* Can we support each other to take the proper course of action, despite the consequences?

In the end, each family must make an intensely personal decision. The dynamics are different in each set of circumstances. What remains is the priority of the family bond. As one pastor put it, "Sometimes pastors have to decide to save their own families, even at the expense of the church. They have to say in essence, 'Church, this is *your* problem. I've got to live with this family, and if I lose them, I don't have another.' "

NINE

COUNSEL FOR RECOVERY

All men may err
but error once committed,
he's no fool nor yet unfortunate,
who gives up his stiffness
and cures the trouble he has fallen in.
Stubbornness and stupidity are twins.

SOPHOCLES

F

ew pastors fall into mistakes by themselves; fewer still recover from them solo. Of the resources for recovery, people are the most precious.

Gordon Weekley spiraled into deep trouble as he removed himself from the help of friends. When drugs clenched his mind and humiliation drained his spirit, Gordon began drifting from city to city.

People in his church still loved him. Some even sought him out on skid row in other communities and the seedy parts of Charlotte. They offered love, counsel, jobs, hope. But Gordon would have none of it. His big mistake with drugs seemed to push him inevitably toward a series of mistakes of lost opportunity.

"I took myself away from the reach of rescuers," Gordon recalls. "I wanted to hide. Though they prayed for me and even found me at times, I frustrated their efforts."

Yet Gordon's behavior cannot be classified as bizarre. How many of us flee from that which would help us! Some perverse human trait drives the lonely into solitude and the stumbling into self-sufficiency. In the midst of a mistake, a further mistake is not realizing we need help.

The Sooner, the Better

"One of the easiest things in the world for me is to convince myself I'm right," observes Dick Lincoln, pastor of Shandon Baptist Church in Columbia, South Carolina. "I easily become blind to real problems because they start small. I'm good at rationalizing my mistakes. That's why I try to see if I'm repeating a mistake. Then I target that problem and get some wise counsel."

When we reach out early, we are more apt to stop the problem before it becomes big. Lincoln looks for the little clues, the repeated slips: Do I regularly miss appointments? Do I often misread people's intentions? Do I repeatedly feel ready to blow up? If so, I need help now.

Alan Taylor could have benefited from counsel before he relocated to Seattle.

"I should have done some investigating outside Broadmoor's search committee," he says. "A probing list of questions for neighboring pastors or denominational staff could have spared me from being blind-sided at the first Session meeting. I knew the type of leadership I had to offer. Even cursory checking could have tipped me off about mismatched expectations. I just assumed the committee understood the church and what it needed. I assumed wrong. I got more surprises in my first three months at Broadmoor than in years of prior ministry."

When Alan began wondering if he should leave Broadmoor, he needed help sorting out his thoughts. The trauma of the first mistake made him wiser. He reached out. Ma Bell smiled at the number of calls he made to friends in ministry, but he found the help he was looking for.

Alan chose those outside Seattle. "I wanted unbiased feedback," he explains. "The people I called weren't friends in town who naturally wanted me to stay or competitors out to get my job. They affirmed my call and gifts, and when the need arose, they weren't afraid to call my bluff. I needed penetrating — even blunt — counsel, not just people to shake their heads and say, 'Ain't it awful!' "

By submitting his feelings to a corrective community, Alan received the wisdom his shell-shocked psyche could not provide.

"Where's my blind spot?" Alan asked. "What am I failing to comprehend?"

One revered role model challenged him. Another friend helped Alan "buy time" by suggesting a short-term ministry at Broadmoor might be God's intention. Alan believed he could tolerate a year or two. Thanks to their encouragement, he hung on.

Reaching out for help makes sense. Through outside observers, pastors may find the problem is not theirs; or they may discover in themselves a particular weakness that sets them up for repeated trouble. And advisers may point out a solution they never thought existed.

Whom to Ask for Help

Alan Taylor's life line was trusted, yet distant, friends. Are they usually the best bet? How about local clergy or professionals? Other staff members? Or even parishioners? Pastors differ on which group provides the best help, and sometimes the answer varies with the problem.

Removed counselors. Alan appreciated the perspective that advisers away from the situation could supply. They were not themselves caught up in the problem. They had nothing to gain or lose by the advice they gave. One step removed, Alan's advisers could see the forest, not just the trees.

Distance can also mean finding counselors who don't "think like a pastor." One pastor says, "When I need input, I don't go to other pastors. I seek out business people whose judgment I trust. They tend to be more hard-nosed than my pastor friends. If I ask them to point out my blind spot, they'll put it on the line. They don't worry so much about what I want to hear as what I need to hear. I appreciate their candor."

Distant counselors also give the expectation of greater confidentiality. A pastor struggling with a frustratingly dispassionate marriage told me, "I don't want to leave my wife. But I need help, and I'm not ready for the congregation to hear about our problem yet. I still think we can make things work, and if we do, it would be better if they never knew. So I can't go to them. I don't even want to seek counseling from local pastors. We're in a small town, so the word would be bound to get out. Even seeing district denominational leaders seems a poor option, because they may view me differently the next time I need a recommendation. So where do I go for help?"

His best bet, if he is determined to keep the situation under wraps, is someone in another community. In such a counselor, he may find assistance without indirectly announcing his problem to the community.

When I began to urge my church in California to consider two worship services, I ran into mixed reactions. Those involved with providing ushers, music, refreshments, and other aspects of the service wondered aloud, "Aren't we pushing things? We're not completely full now. We could fit in more people most Sundays." Another group joined me in thinking we would plateau if we kept the status quo. So I was in a quandary: *Am I pushing too hard? Why do I want to keep moving ahead? If I continue to lobby for the change, will I have a mutiny on my hands?*

I didn't want to ask the other local pastors. It might seem like bragging even to be bothered with such a "problem." So I talked with Dave Wilkinson, a pastor who had faced the same decision prior to a building program in his church in Oroville, California. He knew me and the church well, and he also knew some of the pitfalls I was facing.

With his warm assurance, I decided to press on. We did make the change, and the early service brought in people who hadn't come at 11:00. And with his wise advice, I was able to tiptoe around some of the land mines.

Professional counselors. For all the counseling we do, we pastors are sometimes reluctant to avail ourselves of professional counselors. Burnt-out pastor Richard Kew finally decided professional help was what he needed. "I should have sought counseling and spiritual direction a long time ago," he wrote, "but I guess I was too proud to admit my need. But now, with my life out of control, I put myself into counseling.

"That's one of the best moves I have ever made. Hours of in-depth counseling have brought me face to face with the darker side of my soul and aspects of my personality that have been buried for years. Piece by piece, I am taking them out and examining them so I can discover who I am and what the next step in life will be. The work will probably go on for many months yet, but painful as it is, I am finding myself exhilarated by the richness in me I didn't know existed. Several folk have told me that after a 'death' such as mine comes a resurrection, and maybe the key to that resurrection I desire is the counseling process through which I am passing."

A list of Christian counselors specializing in pastors' problems can be found in the appendix.

Peer counselors. Fellow pastors in the same community have proven to be excellent sources of counsel for many pastors — at least those who have moved beyond competition with one another. A pastor freshly called to a difficult charge quickly warmed up to the other pastors in the local ministerium. Perhaps it was the character of the ministers, but more likely it was his growing awareness of peril. In the previous six years, three other pastors had come to his church and left wounded. He realized he could easily be the fourth.

Over donuts and coffee at the next ministerial gathering, he spilled his story: "My church has always had a strong music program, but it's really in decline now. We're lucky to have a handful in our choir, and we used to fill the loft. When I interviewed, I told the church the choir room was inadequate. The piano was badly out of tune. The folding chairs were bent and rickety. There were no risers to allow everybody to see the director, and the acoustics made it sound like the inside of a sewer pipe. And they seemed to agree.

"So once I was called, I proposed we knock out a wall to an adult Sunday school classroom and 'borrow' about eight feet of space. Then we could put in permanent risers in the choir room, redo the walls and floor to muffle the echo, and get a new piano and furniture. We needed this if our choir is ever going to do well again. I figured if we used mostly church labor, we could do it for under $10,000.

"What do you think happened to my proposal? They tore it apart. You'd think I'd suggested we burn down the church."

One local pastor had been around long enough to see this fellow's predecessors come and go. He spoke first. "What did Barney Cook think about it? Did you ask him before you took it to the board?"

"No, buildings and grounds is not his committee."

"I think you should have asked Barney." Barney was the church kingpin. He donated (some say he still owned) the land the church was built on. His extended family made up 20 percent of the congregation. And his opinion was necessary for anything to fly. His vehement veto meant not only the end of a project but possibly the end of any new pastor's effectiveness. It had happened before — repeatedly.

The other pastors joined in to assist their new member. Since they knew something of the community ways, the history of the church, and the personalities involved, they helped their friend resurrect his idea. First he talked over his idea with Barney. Barney had some concerns to air, but with discussion, they coalesced into "improvements" to the pastor's plan. Then with Barney behind the idea, it sailed through the next board meeting. And Barney eventually donated the new piano!

Barney never became a particularly easy layman to get along with, but the pastor's new understanding of Barney's role in the congregation allowed him to negotiate a peaceful settlement to most subsequent church disputes. In this case, colleagues in town gave the best aid to a scrambling pastor.

In-house counselors. In a culture of privatized religion, sometimes the church is the last to hear about a problem or mistake. "Pastor, I just got fired — but *don't tell the church!*" a church member pleads. "Our son is on drugs — but *don't let on to our Sunday school class!"*

Yet James says, *"Tell* the church!" (5:13–16). It is only when one tells the church that the body can do what Paul commands: "Carry each other's burdens, and in this way you will fulfill the law of Christ" (Gal. 6:2).

What is good for Christians in general usually applies to pastors in particular. In many cases the instinctual *I can't tell the board!* needs to be replaced with *But I've got to.* Of course, when the major aspect of the pastor's mistake involves people on the board, a more disinterested party may give the best help. But pastors are wise not to overlook the aid available in their own church.

Dick Lincoln has set up a pastor's advisory group at Shandon Baptist, a "kitchen cabinet" to head off problems.

"These friends and church leaders are not elected by the church," he says. "They don't have an official capacity in the church government. They carry no weight and cast no votes. I've gathered them with the sole responsibility to advise me. They're wonderful people. I can take any matter to them and get their opinions, and, purposefully, none of them are yes men. Through them I've come to the realization I'm not a bumbler looking for a place to self-destruct. They've helped me discover my strengths and find my own worth — while cautioning me about my weaknesses. They help me see things clearly, usually *before* I stumble into a mistake."

Glen Knecht, Dick's neighbor at First Presbyterian Church, believes a multitude of counselors helps the most, and he's not hesitant to look for them within his Session. He advises: "Listen to your elders. They know more than we often think they do." If elders and board members are chosen for the oversight and leadership of the church, it makes sense to reach out to them for help. God populates his church with gifted people — who can rescue an errant pastor.

The problems with going to the leaders of the church are obvious: confidentiality, biases, a fear of vulnerability. In fact, the board may well *be* the problem. Here are a few reasons *not* to reach out for help from individuals or groups within the church:

— They are substantial participants in or causes of my mistake.

— They have become my adversaries.

— They love me so much they can't be critical.

— Confiding in them would harm the long-term pastor-parish relationship.

— I cannot trust them to hold confidences.

— They are so involved with the matter that unbiased advice is unlikely.

While any of these might be reasons to seek help outside the local church, many times none of these hindrances apply. Sometimes, in fact, we raise objections without substance.

Robert Millen found he had a greater reservoir of understanding and love in his leaders than he'd ever dreamed. Certainly revealing his bisexual lifestyle shocked them, but they stretched a resilient love to include him, despite condemning his sin.

"One of my elders was a right-wing conservative," Robert recalled. "And here I was, some kind of pervert in his book. That man had reason to condemn me. I would have expected him to write me off. Yet this guy still phones me about once a month and asks how I'm doing. He tells me, 'I know how you helped me as my pastor, and you will be my friend until the day I die.' "

Robert's voice cracked, and he was silent for a moment.

"He still cares — who could expect it?"

Robert was surrounded with far more help than he ever imagined possible. He had spent years fighting a terrible enemy alone. He had kept the battle within, and he had lost.

It didn't have to be that way.

TEN

RESTORING YOUR MINISTRY

We mount to heaven mostly on the ruins of our cherished schemes, finding our failures were successes.

A. B. ALCOTT

Yesterday's errors let yesterday cover.

SUSAN COOLIDGE

Animals have a marvelous instinct: after a major trauma, they nest for a while, allowing life to return to normal. For days after our cat's encounter in the neighbor's house, she hung out in the bushes. Katie not only lay low, she walked low, slinking around like a tango dancer. It took about a week for her to become her old self again. But Katie's tactic for recovery made good sense.

Errors inflict grievous wounds — in a pastor's confidence, in a congregation's regard for the pastor, in a church's progress, in interpersonal relationships, in a pastor's family. A kind of depression can set in (sometimes actual clinical depression), making recovery appear only a fleeting hope. *I've blown it; I'm a failure! No one will want me now.*

One pastor recalls his feelings after a devastating church split: "Early on in ministry, my confidence was strong. Every church I was in grew, and I developed a success syndrome. But a denominational change tore our church apart. We decided to part from the denomination, and in that decision I lost many of the people I had pastored for years. We even lost title to the buildings we had built. I began to doubt myself. When two of the elders closest to me opted for the denomination, I felt like quitting." After a few years of turmoil, this pastor recently moved into a beautiful new facility with an enthusiastic congregation. Life goes on.

Wounded pastors sometimes want to crawl into a hole and die. A Band-Aid and a stiff upper lip usually will not patch up the damage imposed by a mistake. Often only a period of recuperation will restore a wounded pastor.

To make the most of mistakes, to survive and even thrive in spite of them, the restoration period is crucial. Any pastor can make mistakes, and most pastors can hobble on after all but the most drastic; the idea is to *grow* through a mistake, to emerge from the experience the better for it.

Pastors who have reflected on their successful recoveries offer several steps toward mending.

Step Back

When mistakes hit, most ministers need a little "space" to think straight — a twenty-four-hour retreat, a weekend away to think and pray, a long drive with one's spouse, a day with close friends to sort out options. By finding time for contemplation, the quality of their decisions rises dramatically. Like counting to ten when you're angry, popping out can eliminate the emotion-laden snap decisions that many live to regret.

As one pastor advises: "Don't make any major decisions when you are under emotional distress. You are least equipped to decide well when your emotions are at play."

Some churches grant a pastor a leave of absence to sort things out. If the mistake was severe, this respite allows the pastor time to work through personal problems, obtain counseling, quiet a trembling heart, regain perspective, and seek the Lord. A prayerful month walking the beach, or a couple of weeks back at the seminary talking with mentors and fellow strugglers, can often work wonders. One who remains enmeshed in a problem may not find a reasonable way out.

Although stepping back briefly may be appropriate for some mistakes, other major mistakes may call for a hiatus from vocational ministry. Robert Millen and Gordon Weekley wisely removed themselves from their prominent pastorates. They understood full well their present unfitness for continued pastoral leadership. Millen's sexual misconduct and Weekley's drugs had destroyed their credentials as leaders.

Neither man was knocked out of life, or even ministry. Their personhood, their individual worth before God, remained intact. Soulful repentance and spiritual rescue salvaged both Robert and Gordon to continue the work of the Lord. But for the immediate future, they had to step down.

John Mark was in the same position following his desertion of Paul and Barnabas in Pamphylia (Acts 13:13). It appears he slunk back to Jerusalem, frightened over the rigors of the apostolic mission and embarrassed by his apparent lack of fortitude. We don't know what he did in Jerusalem for the following months, but we do know he recovered from his humiliation and felt ready to answer a second call to missionary service. Barnabas must have considered this exile sufficient, for he took Mark with him. Paul didn't, even splitting with Barnabas over the matter (Acts 15:36–38). However, later Paul warmly involved Mark in ministry, considering him necessary for his own ministry (2 Tim. 4:11). Ministry can resume after a necessary period of stepping back.

Scale Down

Pastoral ministry stretches incredibly wide in scope. At any given time, a pastor might take on any number of new responsibilities or move the church in any of several directions. Alternatives abound; possibilities pile up. This fact of pastoral life dictates a second course of action for the recovery period: scaling down the scope of pastoral activities.

After an inglorious belly flop, the next dive is not the time to introduce a new twist or an extra flip. The diver needs to reconfirm her ability to enter the water safely and gracefully with a well-executed, familiar dive. It's time to regroup around the basics.

"Any coach knows if your team gets in trouble, you go back

to fundamentals," Alan Taylor explains. "If you lose your perspective, return to what you know." During his stressful days at Broadmoor, Alan found therapeutic satisfaction in the basics — trying to preach his best sermons, visiting, counseling. He did these well and received warm response in return. They gave him needed satisfaction when it was lacking in other areas. These were safe activities, known ruts worn deep by years of practice.

On the other hand, it would have been ill-advised for Alan to launch a TV ministry or an experimental worship service. He was already on unstable ground merely by *being* at Broadmoor. He didn't need to stand on a skateboard.

Attention to pastoral care is also wise because following many ministerial mistakes, the people especially need to know they are loved. The mistake may well have angered, disappointed, or stung them. The personal touch of their pastor soothes sore feelings. Gene Owens, pastor of Myers Park Baptist Church in Charlotte, says, "You've got to lean on your sense of faithfulness to the gospel. Settle on the basics, and keep your pastoral bases covered."

Covering those bases, caring for others, may be the last thing we want to face, caught up as we are in our own failings. Yet such basic pastoral warmth and care are necessary if we plan to remain, and they carry rewards few anticipate.

Many parishioners seem to wait for a reason to again affirm a pastor. Given that reason, they surprise their pastor with love and genuine forgiveness. Owens says, "When my people know I love them and am giving them the pastoral care they deserve, the mistakes I make don't mean as much. They say, 'Oh, he's a jackass, but he's *our* jackass!' "

Scaling down the complexity of ministry and centering on pastoral basics helps stumbling pastors regain their stride.

A Ministry Regained

Sometimes stepping back briefly or scaling down isn't enough. Some pastors require a major recovery period. Stan was one of these.

Stan entered ministry as an associate pastor in Louisville. It wasn't long before he noticed a glaring imbalance in the senior pastor's relationship with his wife.

"It was obvious to everybody," Stan relates. "She'd stuck a ring through his nose. He was nothing more than her errand boy. She'd call him in the midst of a counseling session, and he'd dismiss the counselee and go pick up a loaf of bread for her. It was pathetic, and his ministry suffered for it. People were laughing behind his back. I thought to myself, *That's not going to happen to me! I'm not going to let my family stand between me and my ministry.*"

So Stan decided he would hang his life on Matthew 6:33: "Seek first the kingdom of God and his righteousness, and all these things shall be added to you." He plunged into the ministry and let God take care of his wife, Marj, and their family.

Four years later Stan received what he considered a big break: a call to pastor a Baptist church on the outskirts of Hartford, Connecticut. When he arrived in April, there were thirty-seven people in attendance, but Stan was determined to make it *the* Baptist congregation in New England. By summer the attendance had tripled, and within two years they were averaging four hundred in Sunday school and had plans to construct an auditorium that could seat a thousand.

All this didn't come from wishful thinking. Stan labored night and day to produce the fifteen to twenty who walked down the aisles following a typical Sunday's invitation. More than once he broke down in tears on a Saturday evening because it was too late to call on any more people that week!

Meanwhile, Stan's "widowed" wife wasn't all that thrilled with his success. She had married a bright young man she thought would be her companion. Sure, he was planning to become a pastor, and preachers don't keep bankers' hours. But she didn't expect him to be gone *all* the time. She was raising their children alone, barely feeling Stan's touch as he brushed by with his daily, "I'm off!" Most days she wouldn't see him again until he slipped into bed late that night.

She tried to talk with Stan about his hours.

"Stan, do you realize that in the last month, we've had exactly eight breakfasts, two lunches, and three dinners together as a family? You've been home only one evening, and even then you were phoning the deacons and reading your journal. When's the last time you read to the kids or tucked them into bed?"

She wanted to add, *It's a miracle you found time to have kids,* but she bit her tongue.

"I know I've been busy," Stan murmured, "but what else can I do? I'm a *pastor!*" And he was off to yet another appointment. Part of him wanted to understand her feelings, but another voice cautioned: *It must be Satan's hindrance. He'd like to have you tied down at home rather than winning New England to Christ.* So Stan would try to placate his wife and get on with his real business: growing a thriving church.

After a while Stan noticed that Marj seemed to back off from her pleas for his time. He was relieved that she had finally resigned herself to his schedule. Then one evening Stan dropped by the house to pick up a commentary he needed to complete his sermon. No Marj. *That's odd,* Stan thought. *She didn't say she was going anywhere.* He found the book and camped in his office with it until after midnight. Marj was asleep when he finally tumbled into bed, so he didn't wake her to ask where she had been. By morning he forgot about it.

Over the next several weeks Stan picked up a sense of distance between himself and Marj. She kept her own counsel, even during the brief times they spent together, and a foreign light lit her eyes. But Stan brushed it off. *The kids are happy and fed, the home is clean, and Marj is at church on Sunday. Surely everything's okay.*

But everything wasn't okay. Mark, one of the men Stan had visited during those evenings out, had begun coming to church. Mark was experiencing one of those life transitions that make people more receptive to the gospel. Recently divorced, he was hurting badly over the breakup of his marriage. Stan's concern had touched him, and Mark depended on him for periodic rebuilding.

One evening Mark chanced by Stan's home hoping to talk with him about his loneliness. Stan was out, but when Marj saw Mark's disappointed expression, she invited him in. They talked a couple of hours, and Mark went home feeling much relieved. Marj felt happy that she could help him, and besides, it was nice to talk with an adult after a monosyllabic day with toddlers. She was going to tell Stan about the evening, but he didn't get home until after she went to bed.

Mark and Marj hit it off in the following weeks. He'd often call to chat during the day, or drop by in the late afternoon or evening, on the pretext of catching Stan at home. Stan's mammoth work schedule left plenty of vacant hours for Mark and Marj to fill. What began innocently enough developed into an overly intimate situation. Eventually the affair came to the attention of one shocked workaholic.

After a flurry of How-could-you's followed by a wave of You-don't-understand's, Stan and Marj decided to leave New England. Stan could hardly face the church, and Marj knew she had to move away to stop seeing Mark. They hastily accepted a call to a smaller church in Indiana and tried to piece their life back together. They attended marriage counseling, Stan altered his hours some, and Marj tried to forget Mark.

Five months later, Marj and the kids moved back to Hartford — and Mark. In spite of an overwhelming congregational vote for Stan to remain, he was so devastated from this turn of events, he felt unable to continue in Indiana. He trundled himself off to Charleston for a brief stint as a youth pastor, but even there, some pastors said that as a divorced man he was a disgrace to the ministry. Before long he was back in Louisville working as an investment adviser.

Stan did well and earned good money. He actually became rather wealthy, and he tried to sell Marj again on their marriage. It was dead, however, and for the first time in his life, Stan had to accept bitter defeat.

"The whole thing was extremely painful — more like dying than anything else. I had made evangelism everything; I put aside my wife, my family — everything — to build a church.

Now I was a divorced ex-pastor. It was like denying all I once believed in."

Stan felt guilty for his failed marriage. He was racked with regret and nearly obsessed with getting Marj and the kids back. At that point, Stan would have been an emotional cripple as a pastor.

But time continued on, and lives mend. Stan gained confidence through his work. He found he could succeed, and having proved that, he even mellowed somewhat the irrational drive that was his undoing. He enjoyed a comfortable job and a handsome salary; he met another woman and remarried.

Passing thoughts entered Stan's mind about returning to ministry. *Would I be free to minister again? Did divorce and remarriage cause me to lose my call? Or is God's call permanent? Would anybody accept me as pastor?* But he squelched those thoughts. Stan considered himself "a guy who was down for the count in ministry."

He was doing fine in his secular employment, yet the satisfaction wasn't there. Once he shared his restlessness with his pastor, and the pastor told him, "Stan, you're out of the will of God. You're called to be a pastor, and the way I see it, if you don't get back into the pastorate, it may kill you."

That was all Stan needed. He resigned his job and returned to seminary for more education. While still in school, he was called to pastor a small church in a neighboring rural community, and the same month his wife bore him a son — "Something else I thought I never again would have," Stan says. The people at the church assured Stan he could indeed pastor again.

"I had felt like an outcast with REJECT stamped across my forehead," Stan explains, "but this parish received us so warmly, so graciously, that I felt raised from the dead as a pastor. We had two great years in that loving church."

Stan graduated from seminary, and now is ministering in another congregation, feeling accepted and effective in the pastorate. Like John Mark, Stan dropped out but returned.

"I still struggle with how much to give my family and how much to give my ministry, but I've learned my lesson," Stan states. "Although I may never become as 'successful' as I once thought I had to be, God has given me a dear wife, two sons, and a satisfying ministry. I am blessed."

Change Patterns

Something precipitates a mistake. That something often can be fixed, and the period of recovery is the time to do it.

Stan's pattern of emotional neglect combined with Marj's weakness and sin's opportunity to produce devastating results in his ministry. During the difficult years of Stan's recovery, he began to sort out his priorities. He dealt with the heart of his mistake — his unrelenting drive that caused him to substitute personal ambition for what began as zeal for the Lord's work. When Stan later reentered the pastorate, his first thoughts were on keeping his ministry and home life balanced. Stan used his hiatus from ministry to alter his patterns of living.

Gene Owens says, "After I make a mistake, I need to do my homework. I should have done it before the mistake, but if I didn't, now's the time to study the issues enough to make a better decision next time." That's what Stan did.

Mistakes as sin cry for new patterns to head off temptation. A Sunday school superintendent who was caught embezzling church funds was removed from office. As the church stuck with him and helped him mend his life, they also knew enough to remove him from the temptation of church funds.

A couple of years after his confession, he briefly served as usher. A parishioner, however, halted that with a brief note: "As long as this man is ushering, I'm not going to put any money in the offering. I love him and I'm thankful for him, but to put an offering plate in front of him is like putting a bottle in front of an alcoholic." He didn't usher after that. The church leaders decided he needed to continue to build a pattern of honesty in an area unrelated to finances. Why place him in harm's way?

Rebuild Credibility

The recovery period is a time of reestablishing credibility. The fallen one is being watched. It's definitely a time to mind the store.

Peter, the fallen leader of the disciples, returned to his companions following his denial of Jesus. They were used to his leadership, but I suspect they all were wondering, *Can we trust this guy?* I doubt he regained full trust until his outstanding leadership at Pentecost or his subsequent courage before the Sanhedrin, and these only after Jesus had gently forgiven him and challenged him three times to feed his sheep. Even Peter had to regain credibility.

A negative credibility quotient bankrupts a pastorate. When mistakes drain the account, the ministry goes into a kind of Chapter 11 status until the reserves again accumulate. This time of rebuilding allows little margin for error, and several suspicions demand attention.

Suspect intentions. Perhaps the most damage a major mistake inflicts is upon the church members' perception of the leader's intentions. *Did she mean to speak that way to us? Does he really want to make this church fail? Is ministry a game without rules as far as he is concerned?* When people question our actions, it's hard enough, but when they doubt our very intentions in ministry, that's a credibility crisis. Unless they are assured that we want to please God through our actions, we cannot minister.

One church began to think the pastor was pulling a power play to dismiss an associate simply because they couldn't get along. In truth, however, the pastor had withheld much of the damning information about this associate out of courtesy, not wanting to besmirch his name publicly. But when the associate started making power plays of his own, the pastor had to act.

"I told the people they were deciding about the propriety of the dismissal on insufficient information," he recalls. "Since I didn't want to make a formal announcement, I promised to talk to people privately if they wished. Then I tried to deal with people in small groups, and that didn't work. I needed to talk one-to-one to keep things conversational and let them ask me questions or even argue with me without making a ruckus in a group. Even with all my efforts, people distrusted my motives for some time."

Another pastor trying to handle a doctrinal dispute in his church personally called on people who were upset with the stand he and the board had taken. He patiently explained their reasoning and did his best to educate the people. "I took the 'weird' out of their concept of our decision," he says. It saved the day for that church. People needed to read his intentions for the church and his concern for their opinion.

Suspect morality. Once pastors have rebuilt credibility concerning their intentions, the next step is to model those intentions through their morals.

People never once doubted Gordon Weekley's intentions for the church. They knew his love for it and the effort he had expended to help it prosper. However, when his inability to beat his drug addiction became known, Gordon had to regain moral credibility. Alcohol and drugs rode him to the depths; Jesus Christ rescued him. At least that was Gordon's claim in September 1976. What remained to be seen was if he could stay clean.

For about two years Gordon worked at Rebound, the rescue mission he was in when God redirected his life. For those years Gordon completely abstained from either drugs or alcohol. He worked hard to prove his competence and sincerity.

With recaptured credibility, Gordon has served as executive director of Rebound since 1978, helping transform it into a model agency with a program that truly rescues men and women like himself from chemical bondage.

Sin, even dark, ugly sin, does not necessarily signal the end of ministry; *continuing* that sin does. Whatever sin a pastor has fallen into, the recovery period is the time to show consistent, sterling avoidance. Church members, colleagues, and the public at large must witness a repentant and *changed* person.

Suspect ability. A third area requiring rebuilt credibility is competence, especially when the mistake is one of judgment. When a pastor's competence quotient is low, nothing succeeds like success.

A hard-driving young pastor found himself having difficulties with staff he had not managed properly. A renegade minister of visitation was creating havoc by the disloyal remarks he was making during calls, and the pastor had not handled the situation decisively. When the man began undermining the pastor's plans for a major evangelism festival, the pastor finally stepped in and dismissed him.

Some people sided with the visitation pastor. Others, who didn't particularly care for the man but didn't know the reasons for his dismissal, decried the apparent suddenness of his firing. Most of the leaders stood behind their pastor; they knew the circumstances.

So what was he to do? "I had slipped in the way I originally handled this staff member," the pastor confides. "Even though I inherited him, I should never have allowed him to undermine me the way he did. So what I lacked in prevention, I had to make up in cure.

"I tried to remain as positive as possible. Had I labeled it a gross error, people would have picked up on that. Instead, I went to work in my area of strength. I've always been good with people. I seem to understand them and can get them to understand my position on things. So I began to use those skills. People seemed wary at first, but when they were apprised of our reasons and then saw things were actually going better with this man removed from the scene, the battle was won. They're solid supporters again."

To regain skill credibility, most pastors return to their greatest skills. Chapter seven told of a preacher accused of an affair. He quietly and persistently denied it, and what rescued him was the success of his preaching. He threw himself into that task, and when people responded well to his ministry, the clouds of doubt dispersed. His credibility as a competent pastor was restored.

Take Time

Time, as one humorist put it, wounds all heels. It also heals many of those wounds a mistake occasions.

One of the most beneficial aspects of a period of recovery is the passage of time itself. As the sands trickle through the glass, anger dissipates, memories blur, new impressions intervene, doubts disappear.

Time well used in the restoration process is on the side of the pastor. If pastors and churches are willing to forestall immediate closure, many mistakes will resolve themselves through good will, dogged determination to make things better, and the intervention of the Holy Spirit.

In chapter five we read the beginning of the story of Richard Kew, the Episcopal priest whose well had run dry. His story doesn't end in burnout, with his resignation from ministry and alienation from his wife. Here is how Kew concluded the story:

"Where does my mistake leave me? Right now I don't know. In a couple of weeks I will find myself sitting alone in a pew as an ordinary member of another congregation. There I will have time to lick my wounds and adjust to my 'laicized' state and the single life again. Now my responsibility is to allow the grace of God to work in my life and restore me to wholeness. The rebuilding process will be long and painful, I fear, but I am eager to step out in faith to discover the new me that will surely result from this incredible process."

Two months later, after time intervened, Kew was able to write: "Today is the sixteenth anniversary of my ordination, two months since I resigned my pastorate. What a period of agony and ecstasy!

"The days have been a kaleidoscope of ever-changing patterns. Depression has followed hard on the heels of heady joy, the product of my release from the burden of responsibility. I am at sea, having lost my professional identity, the one that cloaked me through my whole working life. Stripped of wife, family, and parish, and living in rented rooms, I have been forced to look myself squarely in the face and ask some fundamental questions about the man I am and the person I want to be. As bitter as it is, I am attempting to grasp it as a God-given challenge and not an unmitigated disaster.

"The clergy continue to be my greatest source of strength. I could not have survived without their love and care toward me. Their nurture is helping transform my burnout into a fresh beginning."

Then another two months later: "Rereading what I wrote eight weeks ago, I am staggered at the speed with which my life has been restructuring itself. If 'necessity is the mother of invention,' my invention is career counseling. I thought a practice would take months to come together, but it is coalescing more rapidly than I imagined possible, though it is not providing a large enough income yet.

"Perhaps the biggest surprise is to find my wife and me living together again. The investment in counseling has begun to pay off. The tide began turning soon after we separated, although it took time for the necessary breakthrough to happen. We still have a long way to go, but many old, destructive patterns have been broken, and a new style of marriage is being instigated.

"In a few days we will reaffirm our marriage vows in the sight of God, friends, and family. Yet reuniting has not been without its pain, and there are still nights when we weep together. We've each made and continue to work on some significant changes in attitude, so now we can fulfill the vow we will repeat: 'till death us do part.' "

And finally, six months from the fracture: "I almost feel embarrassed to put pen to paper. So many good things have happened since I last wrote, I hardly know where to begin.

"First, I can report our marriage gets healthier week by week. My wife and I enjoy each other's company as never before, and I can't wait to get home in the evenings to be with her. Our children have picked this up and are more settled and content than we have ever seen them.

"But it is on the career front that the biggest changes have taken place. I am about to return to church work — although not parish work. I'm not sure I could handle that again. However, as my faith has returned, refreshed and rejuvenated, I have found it frustrating to look in on church life as an outsider. Soon I will return to the mainstream as executive director of a denominational organization.

"I can't tell you how good it feels to be functioning at full throttle again. I feel less like a middle-aged man recovering from burnout and more like an excited teenager with the whole of life opening up before him. One of my final clients as a career counselor was a burned-out pastor, a gifted and devoted man who has lived beyond his limits for too long and was forced to resign. When he left my office the other day with a brand-new résumé and plans to pursue therapy with a first-rate counselor, there were tears in my eyes. He is where I was less than a year ago. I pray that he may experience the sovereignty of grace that has brought me to a new beginning."

ELEVEN

VICTORY OUT OF DEFEAT

Bad men excuse their faults; good men will leave them.

BEN JOHNSON

Ⅰn a statement worthy of Yogi Berra (who once said, "You can observe a lot just by watching"), one pastor summed up his philosophy of mistakes: "I may not always do what's right, but I won't do wrong." He meant that he may make mistakes, but once he does, he is scrupulous about his conduct as he extricates himself.

Watergate, the classic negative example, showed a whole generation not only how to blunder badly, but how to be bad blunderers. Lies, cover-ups, and betrayed loyalties compounded the initial mistake. What pastors seek in the midst of a mistake is something completely different: a principled recovery, a moral victory in spite of the original mistake.

Taking that moral high ground demands integrity and courage. At just the point when all the world seems to be crumbling, the pastor needs most of all to be stable, to resist petty and vicious retribution, to honor God by modeling faithful behavior. It is perhaps at the point of error that the true character of the pastor shows through.

C. S. Lewis writes in *Mere Christianity*: "Surely what a man does when he is taken off his guard is the best evidence for what sort of a man he is. Surely what pops out before the man has time to put on a disguise is the truth. If there are rats in a cellar you are most likely to see them if you go in very suddenly. But the suddenness does not create the rats: it only prevents them from hiding. In the same way the suddenness of the provocation does not make me an ill-tempered man: it only shows me what an ill-tempered man I am. The rats are always there in the cellar, but if you go in shouting and noisily they will have taken cover before you switch on the light."

When the veneer of success and pleasantness peels off suddenly in a mistake, what's left is the inner person, and *that's* who must find the way out of the problem. Few people can summon character in crisis that wasn't added layer upon layer throughout the rest of life. When the fire alarm sounds at 3 A.M., a city needs firefighters at the station house. That is not the time for a recruitment drive. *Before* a pastor makes a mistake — that's the time to forge the character that will carry him or her through.

Since recovery is aided by character patterns forged over a lifetime, what makes up the character, built during the fat years, that will carry though the lean years? Pastors have indicated several traits.

Openness

"If I am going to retain my people's respect, I've got to remain open-minded, and that means being receptive to negative input," states Gene Owens. "So I make a habit of submitting my views and actions to key people around me. If I am contemplating a decision, I'll ask them, 'Am I wrong? If so, then correct me. Don't let me make a fool of myself!'

"Now to get good feedback, I've got to be able to take what they tell me. I can't get defensive. They'll read that right away, and if they do, I'll only hear from them what I want to hear, not what I need to hear."

Owens is not saying pastors should be so open-minded they become empty-headed. What he does urge is transparency, nondefensiveness. The ability to take criticism or absorb negative opinions not only helps avoid touchy situations but helps mend the breach caused by mistakes. An open pastor is an aware pastor. Harold Englund, who autographs the eggs he lays and holds them up for all to see, exemplifies this stance.

Only the person with something to hide is discovered; only one with a secret is exposed. Those who bury their mistakes often find they are dug up later — dirty, musty, and lie-encrusted. Paul wrote the Ephesians, "Have nothing to do with the fruitless deeds of darkness, but rather expose them. . . . Everything exposed by the light becomes visible, for it is light that makes everything visible" (5:11, 13–14). Transparent pastors throw open the shutters. That character trait, practiced in good times, becomes even more valuable in times of trouble.

Discernment

The wisdom to know when to battle and when to give way, the discernment to know what is truly important and what can slide, can help pastors avoid mistakes or get through the ones they make. Dick Lincoln of Shandon Baptist Church in Columbia, South Carolina, reasons, "I can't afford to waste my silver bullets. I've got to use them on the monsters, not midgets. So I pick my battles carefully. I might not go to war over something like church buses, but I probably would if somebody wanted to cut evangelism from our priorities."

In Terry Muck's research for his book *When to Take a Risk,* he discovered that some pastors tend to view any dispute as theological. In exaggerated terms, if they don't like the cut of your suit, these pastors may consider you a heretic. Pastors like these were forced to leave their congregations more often than those with the discernment to label some misunderstandings a difference of opinion or a personality clash.

Those irenic souls (who yet maintain a corpus of truth that cannot be compromised) find that once they are in a battle, the issues are taken seriously. When they haven't been crying wolf at every occasion, people come running when they do. They have built up reserves of good will from which to draw.

Following a ministry mistake, various courses of action present themselves to a pastor, often at a dizzying pace. *Do I tell Martha and gain her backing, or might she blackball me in Session? What I did wasn't all that dumb, and I might be able to convince people to see my side; should I defend it? Or should I just take the rap? Tom's wrong, but if I point it out will I look petty? I'm not the only one involved in this; should I pin the blame on the others, too?* The wisdom to know the right choices — even to know whom to ask to help decide those right choices — cannot be purchased; it must be developed over years of practice. But this character trait of discernment helps us struggle fairly and wisely as we try to right the error of our ways.

Honesty

Rationalizing is one of the simplest games in town. When we become regular players, we tend to rely on those skills at the time of a mistake. And then we are in deep trouble.

Stan, the pastor whose wife, Marj, had an affair, became particularly adept at rationalizing his time away from his family. After all, he had given them to the Lord to take care of. His ministry was of cosmic importance; people's lives were being saved; the business of the kingdom was getting done.

So, driven by an inward desire to succeed, to build a large church, Stan quit listening to the signals around him about his family's distress. Wrapped around a pledge never to be henpecked, Stan rationalized himself right out of a marriage and, for a time, out of the ministry. Stan failed the honesty test with himself.

Robert Millen exhibited honesty in every area but the one that undid him. He was an upright person. He kept his appointments. He was scrupulous with church finances. But he deceived his trusting wife and everyone else for two long decades. It wasn't until he opened up with devastating honesty that his own soul could quit hemorrhaging from the lies.

His words now trail off into the silence of conjecture: "If I had only gone to my wife sooner . . ."

"If onlys" dog the dishonest.

Honesty also means no hidden agendas. One associate pastor, called in to unscramble a theological fracas left by the departing senior pastor, said: "I had to get positions out into the open, so I got the council to take a stand. We publicized our position, basically saying, 'We believe baptizing children is valid, and this is what we plan to do.'

"Up to this point, the congregation had been abuzz with conjecture and conflicting signals. Once we took our stand, the congregation knew what to expect. I insisted on openness, honesty, no hidden agendas, and it worked. We lost some people, but we got through it once we did away with conjecture and confusion."

Honesty is still the best policy. What is not made clear through direct statements will eventually be dispersed (and likely distorted) by the parish gossip channels. Any number of bizarre interpretations will circulate. Then Murphy's Law kicks in: The more harmful the idea, the more apt it is to be believed.

Integrity

Wrong alternatives abound in the aftermath of a mistake. Cover-ups, finger pointing, run-from-it-all flight — who hasn't considered them? Expediency and shady tactics look terribly appealing to the desperate.

Yet "get through this at any price" is not the name of the game. To evidence anything other than the strictest integrity is to pile iniquity upon error. After our wrong is the time to be downright upright.

"This is precisely the time I need to recognize the difference between the flesh and the Spirit," states Glen Knecht, pastor of First Presbyterian Church in Columbia, South Carolina. "I can usually tell what the flesh is after. The flesh wants me to do things 'right now!' It's impulsive. On the other hand, the

Spirit is more patient. The Spirit keeps coming back patiently with the same idea. If I will take the time to know the mind of the Spirit, then I can head the right direction. Then I need the courage to do what I know is righteous. To know what is right is one thing, to do it another."

The pastor of a large congregation confessed: "I made a dumb decision, and the people in the church started getting after me. Finally I'd had it, and I lost my temper. In no uncertain terms I told a group of our leaders to mind their own business. After I blew up, I stomped out of the room.

"What a mistake! People can't take it when a pastor loses his cool. My vented anger — while it made me feel good at the time — set back my cause considerably. I never want to take that tack again." To keep his anger in check, this pastor set up an exercise program, changed the pace of his day, and vented in minor ways with his wife. "I'm afraid she suffered through some of my pent-up emotions," he recalls.

This pastor lived through his not-so-upright response to his initial mistake. He mended fences and changed his ways. But even so, there remain a few parishioners who won't forget "the day our pastor yelled at us."

Here again lies the reason for searing these character traits into one's soul *before* the disaster. The one who makes integrity a habit will be able to respond with reflexive patterns. Upright decisions and actions will flow more naturally, even in the crunch.

Foresight

"Some people could back themselves into a corner in an igloo!" joked one pastor. "They seem to lack the knack of leaving themselves a graceful exit." No pastor wants to blunder into an inescapable corner. Those with foresight rarely do.

A Baptist pastor reveals his design: "Whenever I have a major decision to make, maybe a direction to move the church or a new program to launch, I build into the process a tactful way out. That way if we get into it and it's simply a bum idea, we can all gracefully retreat. That strategy has saved me from several mistakes that might have toppled me had I been less prepared."

A Presbyterian pastor wanted to change the order of worship, which is not set for him by the denomination but was considered sacrosanct by some of his congregation. His intended changes were not great, but he knew some of the people might grumble. So he got the worship committee to endorse the revision as "an experiment." They told the church they would all try the new order for two months and evaluate it then to determine if it should be kept, modified, or discarded.

The congregation had little difficulty with that process. In fact, most enjoyed "experimenting." The pastor gave the people his best effort during those two months, and the people overwhelmingly approved the changes. Many of those who were originally skeptical found they liked the new way better after the unfamiliarity wore off. The pastor's foresight avoided a mistake.

Although not everything can be calculated, ministers with foresight do what they can to choreograph the exit of a difficult scene even prior to entering the stage. The minister who can dance gracefully off stage after a missed cue saves embarrassment for the whole cast.

One Who Prevailed

Pulling together disparate character traits to successfully resolve a mistake, living through a harrowing time with upright spirit, is never easy, but Mark Huff shows it can be done.

Mark wanted to minister to the singles in Dallas from the time he was called as senior pastor of Tabernacle Assembly thirteen years before. The steel and glass high-rises seemed to contain an inordinate number of equally stark lives. But the church needed a C.E. director and a youth pastor and a song leader and any number of other support staff. One by one Mark had built a solid staff, and the church was finally able to talk about filling a position for ministry to singles.

Mark knew such a ministry demanded a special kind of person. The pitfalls of singles ministry seemed almost as great as the need and the potential. So Mark looked around and inquired among his associates. In a nearby church, he ran into Willie Longmire, who was ministering to a growing singles group. Mark checked with Willie's pastor and received a satisfactory reference. Mark interviewed Willie and hired him within a month.

Willie was sharp. A rather messy divorce about three years back blemished his record, but Mark found himself liking Willie. He figured there must be good justification for Willie's divorce. And besides, Willie wouldn't be on the ordained staff; he would be singles *director*.

"For the first year," Mark recalls, "Willie had a phenomenal ministry, the kind that makes a pastor's eyes dance with delight. He put on high-profile singles seminars that attracted numbers of sharp young folk. These were expensive undertakings with the advertising and speakers' fees and all, and they always seemed to go over budget. But the splash we were making seemed to justify it.

"But after a year or so, when we started analyzing things, we found that Willie was more splash than substance. One of his singles gatherings cost us $8,000, and six months later we could trace only one person who had joined our church. We weren't seeing any Christian return from his ministry. That kind of pattern unsettled us, so I decided to talk with Willie about the matter."

As soon as Mark brought it up, however, it seemed like Willie was waiting for him.

"What are you looking for?" he asked. "Numbers? I can give you numbers if you want, but I'd just as soon be allowed to do my ministry my own way."

Mark tried to explain that he didn't so much want numbers

as spiritual results, people who had clearly benefited from the ministry.

"I didn't get through," Mark said later. Willie left that meeting quite upset, and Mark was left scratching his head.

That was only the beginning of problems with Willie. He had trouble remaining financially responsible. Then he started spreading rumors that he was being persecuted. Since he was so popular, his attitude began to sow dissension in the congregation. Finally, after many rounds that ended in a draw, Mark asked Willie to resign.

But Willie was not one to disappear quietly. While Mark was away on vacation, he got a call from another associate: "I think you'd better come back immediately. You could lose your church." Willie had arranged secret meetings and had mustered a sizable following. They were demanding that either Mark work out his differences with Willie or *Mark* leave the church.

Mark returned and tackled one problem after another. After two months it looked like Willie had found the perfect out: a large church wanted him to be pastor. Mark was ecstatic until Willie announced he had turned down the offer. At this turn, Mark decided he needed a showdown. He convened the church leaders and documented his troubles with Willie. The leaders agreed to fire him. Finally Willie admitted defeat, but he left unwillingly.

The following Sunday, before many knew about the firing, Mark preached on unity, using John 17 as his text. About twelve hundred were present. The news was announced that week, and the following Sunday had nine hundred in attendance.

"I preached three hundred people right out of here," Mark lamented. The next three weeks saw attendance fall about one hundred per Sunday. Eventually attendance leveled off around six hundred.

Willie found another position in another state, but before long a group from Tabernacle Assembly began meeting to start a new church. Two of the wealthiest in that group flew in Willie (who lied to his pastor about his activities for the weekend) to preach at the first service. That group never quite got off the ground, but the instigators eventually joined a weak church about a mile from Tabernacle, gained control, deposed the pastor, and — yes — called Willie. Soon after that, in one week Mark got 105 requests for letters of transfer from people wanting to join Willie's church.

The affair took its toll on Mark and his church. Finances plummeted, morale sagged, membership dropped off, and Mark had to use all his skill just to keep the church afloat. To top that off, people from Willie's church began harassing Tabernacle. They tried to get the church's service taken off the radio. They nearly convinced the health authorities to cancel Tabernacle's hot meals program for the elderly. They wrote letters to Tabernacle's guest speakers trying to get them not to come.

As Mark looks back, he sighs, "I'm not sure I'll ever get over the grief and depression — the fear — from that episode. You can't believe how it undermined my confidence. We're just now pulling out of it as a church, but the wounds are deep."

Wounded Mark was, but in the midst of that trial stemming from his hiring mistake, he tried to maintain a God-honoring posture. "Once I understood what I was getting into with Willie, I resolved to practice three principles," he said.

1. *I will do right, as I understand it, when everything is going wrong, so when things do right themselves again I will have no regrets.* "I had to believe we wouldn't be in this situation forever, and when I looked back on it, I wanted to think I had at least attemped to comport myself as Jesus would have."

2. *I will rid myself of anything that might make me compromise my position.* "I told my family, 'I'm doing what I think is right. Now this may cost me the church. Can we do without our home, the car, college for our daughters?' They stood with me. I had to decide, too, if I could still feel like a man if I were forced out of the pastorate. I gave up the church in my mind so

I wouldn't feel forced to use any means — right or wrong — to stay."

3. *I will not let them just take the church, I will not walk away from it, and I will not run away for another opportunity until all the ends are tied up.* "I wasn't willing to capitulate, nor did I allow myself to quit just because I felt like it. That's an awful temptation. Not allowing another juicy opening to lure me away meant I had to stay and fix this mess. Those other opportunities look all the better when the home church is a mess, but I didn't want to give up for the sake of my own convenience."

These resolves worked for Mark, and they kept him and the church on the high road. Mark's still at his church, and though he and the church often grieve the fight, they hold their heads high. Mark and Tabernacle Assembly won the moral victory. The church is again vigorous.

Willie? He lasted about eighteen months at the nearby church and vacated for parts unknown. Sadly, his church has just about followed him into oblivion.

TWELVE

AMAZING GRACE

There's no defeat, in truth, save from
  within;
Unless you're beaten there, you're bound
  to win!

HENRY AUSTIN

Thy part is with broken saber
To rise on the last redoubt.

LOUISE IMOGEN GUINEY

I

n 1928 Alexander Fleming made a careless mistake, which wasn't his custom. He had completed university and medical school with academic distinction and served with honor in the army medical corps in World War I. Then he returned to research and teaching at the Royal College of Surgeons, trying to find antibacterial substances that would be nontoxic to animal tissues. And he had achieved a measure of success.

While researching influenza, however, he somehow contaminated a staphylococcus culture dish with mold and ruined the culture.

That uncharacteristically careless act resulted in what has been termed a "triumph of accident and shrewd observation," for Fleming noticed the mold had produced a bacteria-free spot in the previously thriving staphylococcus colony. Upon further investigation, he observed the mold produced a substance that prevented staphylococcus growth, even when diluted eight hundred times. He christened that substance *penicillin*, and medicine has not been the same since.

For his mistake, Fleming was knighted, and in 1945 shared the Nobel prize. Because of Sir Alexander Fleming's mistake, hundreds of thousands of people have been healed and even saved from death. We could use more mistakes of that sort.

When another man was but seven years old, his family was forced out of their home on a legal technicality, and he had to begin working to help support them.

At age nine, his mother died.

At twenty-two, he lost his job as a store clerk. He wanted to go to law school, but his education wasn't good enough.

At twenty-three, he went into debt to become a partner in a small store. Three years later his business partner died, leaving him a huge debt that took years to repay.

At twenty-eight, after courting a girl for four years, he asked her to marry him. She said no.

At thirty-seven, on his third try, he was elected to Congress, but two years later he failed to be reelected.

At forty-one, his four-year-old son died.

At forty-five, he ran for the Senate and lost.

At forty-seven, he failed as the vice-presidential candidate.

At forty-nine, he ran for the Senate again, and lost.

At fifty-one, he was elected President of the United States.

Abraham Lincoln is considered by many to be the greatest leader this country has ever produced. Yet in his day, even as president, many considered him a failure.

Today in schoolrooms across the United States, students study the Gettysburg Address as a triumph of composition. Yet in 1863 it was greeted with hostile reviews. The *Patriot and Union* said of his speech: "The President succeeded on this occasion because he acted without sense and without constraint in a panorama that was gotten up more for the benefit of his party than for the glory of the nation and the honor of the dead. . . . We pass over the silly remarks of the President; for the credit of the nation we are willing that the veil of oblivion shall be dropped over them and that they shall no more be repeated or thought of."

In a like manner the Chicago *Times* wrote: "The cheek of every American must tingle with shame as he reads the silly, flat, and dish-watery utterances of the man who has to be pointed out to intelligent foreigners as the President of the United States."

What a failure this bumbling president must have been! We could use more failures like him.

To Err Is Human; to Benefit Is Grace

Not all mistakes cause failure, and not all failures remain so. Amazing grace often intervenes.

William A. Ward observed:

"Failure should be our teacher, not our undertaker. . . .

"Failure is delay, not defeat. . . .

"It is a temporary detour, not a dead-end street."

The mistakes a pastor makes along the way, even the big ones, can usually be weathered, even though they leave their marks. Often the imprint of those hard mistakes becomes a source of character far surpassing anything learned in soft prosperity.

So should we err that character may abound? No, but once an error is committed, grace may guide the course toward a positive outcome.

Why do some pastors crumple under the effects of a mistake, while others gain backbone and grow strong through the process? Perhaps the answer lies in the attitude of living through mistakes in the presence of God. Solomon wrote: "My son, if you accept my words and store up my commands within you, turning your ear to wisdom and applying your heart to understanding, and if you call out for insight and cry aloud for understanding, and if you look for it as for silver and search for it as for hidden treasure, then you will understand the fear of the Lord and find the knowledge of God. For the Lord gives wisdom, and from his mouth come knowledge and understanding" (Prov. 2:1–6).

In pastor after pastor I interviewed for this book, I observed wisdom and sensitivity engendered by past mistakes. As they told their stories, their eyes and voices indicated the pain they had borne, the guilt, the humiliation, the sorrow. But for the most part, their lives and ministries evidenced stiffer resolution and greater clarity of purpose. They had learned to place their mistakes in perspective, gain wisdom from the experience, and live with the grace of God.

The driven achiever was wounded, and thus made more human, more compassionate with the pains and struggles of his parishioners. The cocky theorist had his misconceptions pierced, but deflated, more vulnerable, he has a much more effective ministry. The hesitant soul unsure of his ideas and afraid of every step fumbled the ball anyway, but found he could survive the experience and even learn from it. He's less timid now. The cold husband now cherishes his wife. The fiercely independent pastor now values his colleagues. And on and on.

Ministry mistakes may leave their scars — broken marriages, wasted years, lowered horizons, injured relationships, misdirected congregations, a snickering world — but they also can sharpen the mind and temper the soul. The Comforter intervenes to help pastors learn from mistakes and grow through them. Those who emerge from mistakes with their attitudes softened and their character honed are the better for their testing.

The Greening of a Pastor

Bob Rhoden arrived in Richmond, Virginia, in 1969 with a Bible in his hand and a dream in his heart. Fresh from school at twenty-six years of age, he intended to establish a great church to minister to folks on Richmond's growing fringe. West End Assembly of God got off the ground with twelve people, but it's closer to one hundred times that figure today. In the intervening years, Bob made some mistakes and learned a few lessons. He tells about the major one:

As I look back on my early days of ministry, I must confess I didn't really know how to pastor. I didn't come into ministry with much background. I hadn't grown up the son of a pastor or enjoyed any great mentor. My schooling was not in the area of pastoring. So whatever I learned, I had to gain by trial and error.

But lack of background didn't keep me from grand ambition. I wanted to be successful, and the only measure for success I understood was numbers. And starting out with a mere handful does tend to make a crowd look pretty good.

I began to schedule the kinds of events that would draw an audience. My method was to book as many as I could. Around the big events, I tried to weave the other elements of ministry, like preaching and evangelism and discipleship. Before long, we developed a reputation as an exciting place to be. People started coming to see if our reputation was true.

In a city with three or four churches using this kind of event programming, you end up with a crowd of followers who "want to be where the glory comes down." People flock to one church or another in search of excitement, not commitment. And that's the major problem.

I patterned West End Assembly as a *Christian center*, not a church. A center is a place where attention is focused on the needs of the individuals rather than on what they can give to God. There's not much said about involvement; the focus is on "what I can get from this meeting."

Our ministry was built on false expectations. People came with the idea that this meeting was going to be bigger and better than the last one. They were pumped up, wondering, *What's going to happen tonight?* So the church staff found itself on edge, constantly having to provide a better extravaganza, a greater thrill, a steeper emotional ride — for basically uncommitted people.

At the time, I thought I was building a church. I was doing the things that brought people. The institution was growing. We were definitely out of the tiny stage and on our way to bigness. But my understanding of the church had not been refined. We were on our way, but I got us off on the wrong foot.

We had no way of integrating people into the life of the church. There was little sense of family, little commitment. For instance, I couldn't even depend on consistent attendance. If I didn't promote some exciting event any given week, practically nobody would show up. If some unknown singer was scheduled, only fifty people would come, rather than the five hundred who would come for a big-name entertainer. We had a flock of groupies looking for the best show in town.

When we started hiring staff, we discovered the people didn't actually consider our staff their pastors. Merely attending the events at our church didn't give them a sense of being under our care. They didn't pay their share of pastoral salaries. They would leave a good offering at an event, but they weren't prepared to underwrite a church program.

Then we made another strategic mistake. Because we had so many people coming to our events, we decided to emphasize what we thought was our strength. We concluded we needed more room. The leaders and I thought the right way to build would be to pay as we go. We tried to sell our decision to the congregation, giving them all the reasons why this was the proper course. We came up with projections of growth and income. We showed how we absolutely had to have the building and how the new people it brought in would help us pay for it.

But the people weren't with us. Many said we were presumptuous and unrealistic. But we went ahead anyway, thinking we knew better. It wasn't long, however, before the projected costs of this new building escalated beyond our ability to pay.

By this time, however, we were deeply into the project. We had to back off from our original projection. The leaders agreed we needed to take out a loan to pay for part of the building costs. Since we had given the original sales job such a spiritual flavor — "*God* has told us to do this!" — we then came across rather poorly, saying, "Well, now, maybe God didn't tell us to do it." With all this backpedaling, our credibility as wise leaders was shot.

We invited some of the high-powered critical members to meet with the elders and deacons. We said, "Let's get together and talk this through." The meeting turned out to be a barroom brawl as they told us flatly, "You need to file for bankruptcy and put the church in the hands of a receivership."

I arched my back and declared, "We're not going to do that!" Tempers rose. The meeting degenerated from there.

One of the critics finally said to a deacon, "Do you want to step outside and settle it?" It was not an idle threat.

An elder who is an FBI agent happened to be sitting between the two, and he stood up and said, "Hey! This is no place to talk like that."

The deacon who had been challenged said, "I'm leaving!" and walked out. The other guy remained, red faced. He muttered something like, "I shouldn't have said that. I probably spoke too soon," although it was hardly an apology. We tried to smooth things over, but I was so upset I don't even remember now how the meeting ended, though I remember being there until 3 A.M.

Our problem had become enmeshed with personalities. People were as upset with each other as they were with the crumbling building plans, and I had to take blame for the fiasco. I had given members the sense that I was not a good financial manager. It was true; I had not managed the building project well. The disgruntled people, some of our heaviest contributors, saw me as the incompetent president of the company, and I think, at that point, some were actually anxious to see me fail so the church would fall into different hands.

Everything was on the line — my ministry, our vision for the church, even the existence of the church — and we knew it.

The church was walking through the motions of a plan they considered *my* dream, not their own. People began coming to church not to grow spiritually but to find out how much money we owed. This state of affairs was partly a function of bad decisions, but more fundamentally of people's expectations for the church — what I had unfortunately led them to believe a church was about.

How do we get out of this? I wondered. I had to come up with some kind of solution. Our church has a saying: "If we do the natural, God will do the supernatural." So we did the natural.

At the time, I had two other staff pastors and two lay elders on our leadership team. When we gained some presence of mind, we started to ask, "Okay, how is God at work in this mess?" The five of us decided to get apart for a retreat to analyze what was going on. We knew we couldn't keep grabbing at air.

On that retreat, we didn't actually come up with the center-versus-church idea, but we did realize we needed to do something about commitment. Over the next few weeks we slowly came to the conclusion that our church was nothing but a center, a gathering place for people not integrated into the life of the congregation.

We started talking about commitment with the members and leaders at every opportunity. We made it our theme for the year. I preached on commitment, and we did Bible studies about it. I'd like to say our brilliant revelation was met with resounding cheers, but actually it was very unpopular. Our attendance decreased when we stopped having so many special guest speakers. But rather than thinking "How many people will this speaker bring in?" our criterion was "How will the speaker further the purpose of our church?"

Still the building problem hung over our heads. At one meeting our associate pastor volunteered, "You know, if we had something that could get our eyes off this and onto something more significant, we would be better off." The idea caught us, and we started throwing around wild ideas. Finally we settled on a plan only Christians would consider: We agreed to help a congregation in the Dominican Republic by building a church *for them* — we who couldn't even agree on our own building!

When you think about it, it's ridiculous. There we were, owing more money than we thought we could find to build our own church, yet we were considering building one for someone else. All the leadership agreed on it. All the people, too. It didn't matter which side of our building problem people were on, they liked the idea.

With little effort, we got twenty people to go, paying five hundred dollars apiece for plane tickets. The church quickly raised nearly twelve thousand dollars for the Dominican building. The people went and the church prayed, and it was a marvelous success.

I think the genius of the project was that it was *right*. It was a good thing to do. It drew us together for a manageable problem that was focused outside our own petty bickering. The prevailing notion seemed to be: "Here is a common project we can work on, and let's believe somehow we are going to get our problems taken care of in the midst of it."

We put up our own building after that and got it paid for promptly. And we did it with a new sense of unity. In the months following that experience, we came up with a church theme: *Touching People*. As I reoriented my organizational model from a Christian center to a loving, committed church, we found we could grow together as a *family*.

We did lose some people. The man who challenged the other to a fight left along with about thirty-five others six months later.

Our church has nearly doubled since that time. We're even thinking of expanding our facilities again, and the best part about that is, all the decisions to this point have been unanimous!

Bob Rhoden came close to seeing his dream for the church crumble, if not his very call. He had to shoulder responsibility for a cluster of mistakes that brought him to that point. But what I found in Bob, and witnessed over and over again in other pastors' stories, is that most pastors don't remain locked in the grief of their mistakes.

Bob took some proper steps, and the Holy Spirit met him

more than halfway. Renovation was the outcome. But even *renovation* is a weak word, for it implies Bob returned to his previous state following the mistake. Bob was not brought back to an existing condition; he was pushed forward to a new level of maturity in ministry. And the church Bob brought through his trial emerged, with him, the better for it.

It doesn't happen only for Bob — or Stan or Josh or Mark. The apostle Paul, that dauntless first-century pastor, well understood the path a life can take after even the worst of mistakes. Late in life he wrote, "Not that I have . . . already been made perfect, but . . . one thing I do: Forgetting what is behind and straining toward what is ahead, I press on toward the goal to win the prize for which God has called me heavenward in Christ Jesus" (Phil. 3:12–14).

That's what God does in a life. That's how he works.

Mankind devolves to the Flood (obviously the end) yet grows again through Noah's seed. Abraham, whose offspring would be as uncountable as the stars in the heavens, grows ancient without a single legitimate heir (ha!) but eventually becomes the father of a great nation. Jesus Christ dies (cruel twist) but is raised the absolute Conqueror of death and King of Kings. God is the master of imparting winning spin to tricky shots. This same God can rescue us from the effects of errors any of us may perpetrate in ministry.

The psalmist writes: "As a father has compassion on his children, so the Lord has compassion on those who fear him; for he knows how we are formed, he remembers that we are dust" (Ps. 103:13–14).

Dust indeed, but cherished dust — dust "a little lower than the heavenly beings and crowned . . . with glory and honor" (Ps. 8:5).

The dust makes mistakes, but the Lord, the Redeemer of dust, has a different outcome in mind: perfection, transformation, Christlikeness. God wants us to accomplish all he plans for us, and the path to that accomplishment leads us through — and beyond — mistakes.

APPENDIX

In *Counseling Christian Workers* (Word, 1986), Louis McBurney notes that most denominations have means to provide confidential assistance to pastors seeking counsel. In addition, he lists several nondenominational centers geared for pastors' needs. Following is a partial list.

Barnabas Ministries
P.O. Box 37179
Omaha, NE 68137
(402) 895-5107
Director: Dale Frimodt

Center for Career Development and Ministry
70 Chase Street
Newton Center, MA 02159
(617) 969-7750
Director: Harold Moore

Chalet I
90 Trail West Village
Buena Vista, CO 81211
(303) 395-6423
Director: Hazel Goddard

Fairhaven Ministries
Rt. 2, Box 1022
Roan Mountain, TN 37687
(615) 542-5332
Director: Charles Shepson

Laity Lodge
P.O. Box 670
Kerrville, TX 78028
(512) 896-2505
Director: Howard Hovde

Link Care Center
1734 West Shaw Avenue
Fresno, CA 93711
(209) 439-5920
Director: Brent Linquist

Marble Retreat
139 Bannockburn
Marble, CO 81623
(303) 963-2499
Director: Louis McBurney

The Midwest Career Development Service
2501 North Star Road, Suite 200
Columbus, OH 43221
(614) 486-0469
           and
1840 Westchester Boulevard
Westchester, IL 60153
(313) 343-6268
Director: Frank C. Williams

The Alban Institute
4125 Nebraska Avenue NW
Washington, D.C. 20016
(202) 244-7320
Director: Loren Mead

The Buford Foundation
P.O. Box 9090
Tyler, TX 75711
(214) 561-4411
Director: Fred Smith, Jr.

The Center for Ministry
7804 Capwell Drive
Oakland, CA 94621
(415) 635-4246
Director: John R. Landgraft

Uphold Ministries
8787 East Mountain View Road, #1055
Scottsdale, AZ 85258
(602) 998-3307
Director: Ed Pittman

Villacita Pastoral Counseling
17576 County Rd. 501
Bayfield, CO 81122
(303) 884-2901
Director: Jerry Brown